CREATE YOUR OWN
NATURAL
DYES

CREATE YOUR OWN
NATURAL
DYES

Kathleen Schultz

 Sterling Publishing Co., Inc. New York

DEDICATION

To John and to Jeffrey, for their patience, understanding, and encouragement.

First paperback printing 1982
Copyright © 1975 by Sterling Publishing Co., Inc.
Two Park Avenue, New York, N.Y. 10016
Distributed in Australia by Oak Tree Press Co., Ltd.
P.O. Box J34, Brickfield Hill, Sydney 2000, N.S.W.
Distributed in the United Kingdom by Blandford Press
Link House, West Street, Poole, Dorset BH15 1LL, England
Distributed in Canada by Oak Tree Press Ltd.
c/o Canadian Manda Group, 215 Lakeshore Boulevard East
Toronto, Ontario M5A 3W9
Manufactured in the United States of America
All rights reserved
Library of Congress Catalog Card No.: 74-31708
Sterling ISBN 0-8069-7576-8

Contents

Before You Begin 7
1. Getting Started with Natural Dyes. 9
   Equipment . . . Terminology . . . Water . . .
   Dye Sources . . . Preparing the Dyestuff and Dye
   Liquor . . . Basic Dye Recipes . . . Onion Dye . . .
   Coffee or Tea . . . Wild Onion Grass, Rhododendron and Spinach Leaves . . . Marigold or Dandelion Flower-Heads . . . Sumac Berries . . . Adding Mordants to the Dye Liquor . . . Basic Mordant Recipe . . . Preparing the Yarn . . . Preparing the Dye-Bath . . . Dyeing the Wool . . . Rinsing the Wool . . . Natural Loom—Natural Dye
2. Exploring with Natural Dyes 24
   Collecting Barks and Other Hard Sources . . .
   Collecting Roots . . . Collecting Cones and Hulls
   . . . Preparing the Dye . . . Water . . . Mordanting the Wool . . . Mordant Recipes for One Pound of Wool . . . Chrome Mordant . . . Tin Mordant . . . Iron Mordant . . . Basic Mordant Procedure . . . Labels . . . Dyeing Already-Mordanted Wool . . . Batches . . . Tints. . . Judging the Results . . . Hooked Rug
3. Experiments with Natural Dyes 48
   Fade Test . . . Wash Test . . . Selecting and Storing Dyestuff . . . Preserving Dyes . . . The After-Mordants . . . Blooming . . . Saddening . . . Greening . . . Glauber's Salt . . . To Set Dyes with Tannin Content . . . Vinegar . . . Working with

Handspun and Unspun Wool . . . Washing Fleece
. . . Scouring the Wool . . . Drying Wool . . . Top-
Dyeing . . . Sectional Dyeing . . . Duplicating Color
. . . Pots . . . Notebook . . . Group Projects with
Natural Dyeing

4. Ancient Dyes—History and Recipes 70
Ancient Dyes You Can Use . . . Cochineal . . .
Madder . . . Logwood . . . Indigo . . . Quercitron
. . . Cutch or Gum Catechu . . . Pokeweed . . .
Top-Dyeing to Create Black . . . Top-Dyeing to
Create Green . . . Top-Dyeing to Create Purple

5. Guide to Dye Sources and Mordants 80
Red and Purple . . . Blues . . . Yellow . . . Yellow-
Green and Green . . . Orange and Gold . . .
Ochre . . . Brown and Tan . . . Grey

Glossary 86
Suppliers 90
Metric Conversions 94
Index 95

Acknowledgments

The author and publishers would like to thank all who have helped during the preparation of this book, with particular thanks to Paul A. DeAngelis and Harold D. Friedlander for their proofreading and editing advice; Peter Sereico for his technical assistance in the field of chemistry; and the art students of James Caldwell High School for the examples they provided.

Before You Begin

Making a dye is as easy as boiling a fresh vegetable. Have you ever noticed the color of the water after you cook fresh spinach or beets? That water is a natural dye, and boiling is the basic procedure in extracting a dye color from plants. That is what natural dyes are all about.

The techniques are fun, simple to learn, and fascinating to explore. Most of the equipment you need is ordinary kitchenware, so you will not have to make much of an investment to try this ancient craft. Certainly the dyes are free: color is everywhere in nature and readily available all year round. You can even extract color from hard substances, such as bark or pine cones.

When you learn about natural dyes, you become involved with nature on a new and exciting level. You find yourself looking at plants not only for their physical beauty, but also for the colors they might yield in a dye. Nature offers a wide spectrum, yet the colors of a forest or field never clash. Capture these colors and use them in your own projects. No one else in the world is using exactly the same colors you have created and whatever you do with the dyed yarns, your work will be expressive and unique.

All the measurements in this book are American. For metric equivalents, see page 94.

Illus. 1. Here is the simple equipment you will need to get started making your own natural dyes.

1. Getting Started with Natural Dyes

Equipment

Here is the only equipment you will need to get started with natural dyes, and you probably have most of the tools and utensils in your kitchen already. The kitchen serves as an excellent workshop, too, but all you really must have is a heat source (a hot plate will do), and some running water.

You will need an *enamel* kettle that holds at least 4 gallons of water (kettles made of iron, aluminum, or copper affect the final dye color). A small weight scale is helpful but not essential; one that registers the weight in grams rather than ounces is easier to work with. If your skin is sensitive or if you worry about stains on your hands, wear a pair of rubber gloves while you work.

- Enamel Kettle—to make the dye and dye the yarns
- Rinse Bucket or Tub—to rinse the yarns and strain the dye
- Strainer or Cheesecloth—to separate the dyestuff from the dye
- Spoon or Smooth Stick—to stir the dye and wool
- Measuring Cup or Gram Scale—to measure the dyestuff and mordants
- Heat Source—stove or hot plate
- Alum and Cream of Tartar—the mordant
- One Pound of Wool—16 ounces, unbleached and dry
- Optional Equipment—indicator paper, thermometer, rubber gloves, pot holders, colander

Illus. 2. You will find sources for your dyes no farther away than your refrigerator or back yard.

Terminology

Generally, when we talk about natural materials before they are gathered, we call them dye sources; after they are gathered and in hand, we call them dyestuff or dyematter. After they produce the dye, they are "bulk material." The dye liquor is the concentrated dye; the dye-bath, the diluted liquor with enough water added to make 4 gallons.

Water

At one time, rain water served as a perfect water source for dyeing, but due to air pollution, today's rain water is no more desirable than tap water. Ordinary tap water varies in its degree of acid, alkaline, and mineral content, and when you work with natural dyes, these qualities will affect your results. It is simple to determine what type of water you have, and even easier to neutralize it and soften it. (See page 30.)

Dye Sources

Almost all plant life produces a color, so there are natural dye sources all around us: the coffee or tea we drink; herbs, spices, and the fresh vegetables we use. Don't let the required quantities of dye sources frighten you; they are not so difficult to collect. The chart below shows the quantity of some common materials you need to dye one pound of yarn. Choose one convenient to you for a trial project.

Color	Source	Amount (Approximate)
Yellows	Dandelion flower-heads (fresh)	12 quarts
	Marigold flower-heads (fresh)	12 quarts
	Outer onion peels	8 quarts
Greens	Rhododendron leaves (chopped)	8 quarts
	Spinach leaves (chopped)	4 pounds
	Wild onion grass or tops (chopped)	8 quarts
Browns/Tans	Ground coffee	1 pound
	Tea	1 pound
	Sumac berries	4 quarts

Hint: Some grocers will let you take outer onion peels free (you are cleaning his bin). Overripe fruits and vegetables are often given away or sold inexpensively. Flowers and leaves are not difficult to collect—it just takes a little time—and many unwanted weeds give beautiful results.

Preparing the Dyestuff and Dye Liquor

Collect the dyestuff at its peak ripeness in order to extract the strongest colors. Wash the leaves, plants, and berries and then cut them into 3-inch pieces approximately. Cleaning them removes dirt which can dull the color, and cutting them exposes more plant cells which decreases the dye extraction time. Soaking the dyestuff in water for several hours or even overnight also decreases the cooking time.

When you use dye sources that produce yellow or red colors, you can obtain brighter results by soaking them for a long period, then cooking them for a relatively short time at a low simmer of about 170°F. (about 77°C.) instead of the usual 190°F. (about 88°C.). Heat destroys anthocyanins, the pigments which produce reds and yellows in flowers and plants.

To make the dye liquor, simmer the dyestuff in at least 2 to 3

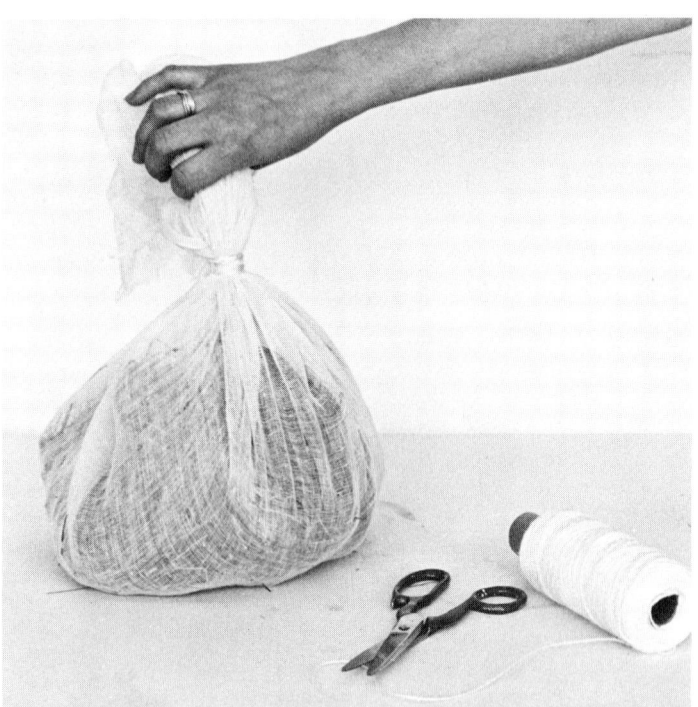

Illus. 3. When using a dye source such as coffee, tie it up in a cheesecloth sack, leaving ample cloth at the top to serve as a "handle."

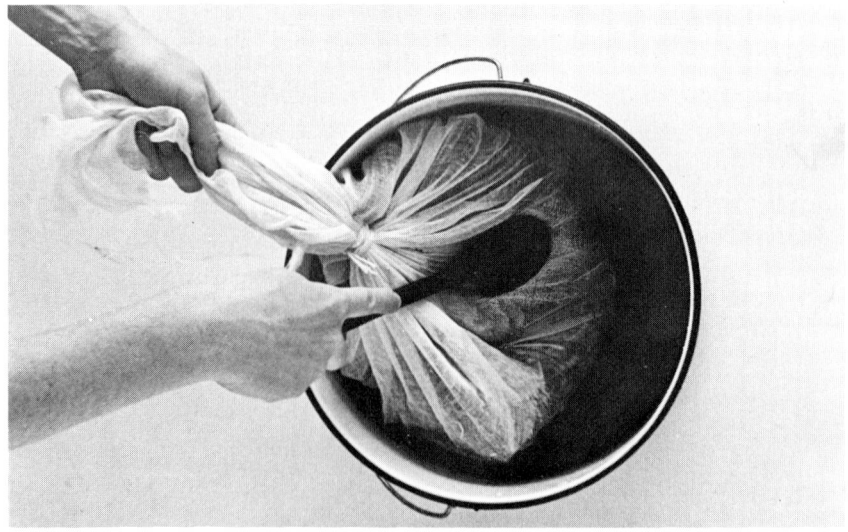

Illus. 4. Work the sack in the water the same way you would a tea bag. Use a wooden spoon for pressing.

Illus. 5. If you let your dyestuff float in the water, use a colander to strain the bulk material from the liquor.

gallons of water; the time will vary with the source. Generally, the more solid the source, the longer it takes to extract color. Leaves, hard berries (such as sumac), and plant parts usually take one to two hours. Flower-heads and peels take no more than one hour. When you make the dye, start with cold water, slowly bring it to a simmer, and hold it at that point for an hour or so until the water ceases to grow darker in color. If water should evaporate while the dye is being made, add hot water to bring it to its original level.

Some sources, such as ground coffee or tea, should be tied in a cheesecloth or muslin sack. Use only white cord; colored string may contaminate the dye. If you use the sack method, work the bag by pressing down on it with a wooden spoon or stick as you would a tea bag, to encourage the dye to permeate the water. When the dye is ready, simply remove the sack and you are ready to enter the yarn.

Another alternative is to let the dyestuff float freely in the water. This method works best for bulk material, such as leaves. In this procedure you don't have to work the dyestuff, but be sure to strain away the bulk before you dye the yarns.

Basic Dye Recipes

Here are specific recipes for some common dyestuffs; each one of them produces enough dye to color one pound of wool. Each recipe starts with 2 to 3 gallons of cold water, and you need to simmer or boil, as indicated, for at least one hour in order to extract the dye.

Onion Dye

Measure out a generous 8 quarts of onion peels and place them in the water. You can use red or yellow peels, or a combination of both. Red onions make the color a little redder or warmer. Bring them to a low simmer and hold at that heat for about an hour, or until the water does not get any darker. Then strain the peels away from the colored water with a wire strainer or colander. What is left is the dye liquor.

Coffee or Tea

If you use coffee or tea, tie it in some muslin or cheesecloth, as mentioned before and shown in Illus. 3; otherwise you would need to strain it away before entering the yarn. Immerse the sack, and boil for at least an hour. Work the sack with a spoon now and then to force the color out of the bag and into the water. When the dye is ready, remove the sack. If any dyestuff is loose in the water, strain it with cheesecloth or a wire strainer. Both coffee and tea contain a substance called "tannin," and the strength of it varies with the brand of coffee or tea you use. The higher the tannin content in the dye, the browner the final color will be. Tannin often causes wool to darken with age.

Wild Onion Grass, Rhododendron and Spinach Leaves

Use these leafy dye sources while they are fresh for stronger and brighter colors. After you gather them, clean and cut them into 3-inch pieces approximately. You may soak them in water for several hours, or even overnight to reduce cooking time, or simmer them immediately. Since they are relatively soft, soaking is not really necessary. Put them in the water, slowly bring them to a simmer and hold at that point for at least an hour or until you see no deepening of the color of the water. Then strain away the bulk from the dye liquor. The extraction time varies

Illus. 6. Chop freshly gathered and cleaned onion grass into pieces approximately 3 inches long.

with these dye sources: rhododendron leaves and onion grass are a bit more resistant to color extraction than are spinach leaves.

Marigold or Dandelion Flower-Heads

Flower-heads yield their brightest colors when they are in full bloom. You may wait until they are overripe, but the colors of

Illus. 7. Be sure to pick dandelions at the height of their bloom to achieve the brightest possible dye.

Illus. 8. Sumac berries are bright red and become fully ripe by early fall, which is the time to pick them.

the dye made from them will not be as bright. You don't need to wash them unless they are noticeably dirty. Soak them in cold water for a few hours or overnight to decrease the time you must expose them to heat. Be sure to heat them at a low simmer; a fast boil will change or darken the final result. If you pre-soak, simmer for an hour. If you don't pre-soak, simmer until the dye color does not deepen. Strain away the flower-heads.

Sumac Berries

Rhus glabra (smooth) or *Rhus typhina* (staghorn) are both non-poisonous and can be recognized from their red berries. Poison sumac, *Rhus vernix*, is a shrub which usually grows in swamps and shady areas. Its berries are greyish-white and not recommended for dyeing.

Pick the berries when they are fully ripe, in the late summer or early fall. Bruise them and the berry stalks with a hammer and cut the stalks into 3-inch pieces approximately. Soak them for a few hours before cooking. Then boil for one hour and strain away the bulk. Because sumac has a high tannin content, the dye may darken with age.

Adding Mordants to the Dye Liquor

Mordants are vital to the natural dye process. They are chemicals that fix the dye on the yarn and make the color permanent. They also help yarn absorb the new color. Of all the popular mordants, alum and tartar are most easily purchased. Alum is a metallic salt that is available in two forms: aluminum potassium sulphate and aluminum ammonium sulphate. The first is generally used by artist-craftsmen, but the second works just as well and you may purchase it in any pharmacy. Cream of tartar, or tartaric acid, which you may use for baking, brightens the color and keeps the yarn silky; you may buy it in many food stores. Alum and tartar together make up the basic mordant recipe. Measure the ingredients carefully since too much alum makes the yarn sticky.

Basic Mordant Recipe

Dissolve 3 ounces of alum into $\frac{1}{2}$ cup of warm water, and add it to the dye liquor.

Dissolve one ounce of cream of tartar separately in $\frac{1}{2}$ cup of warm water, and add it to the dye liquor.

When you use this basic recipe, the dye process and the mordant process take place simultaneously.

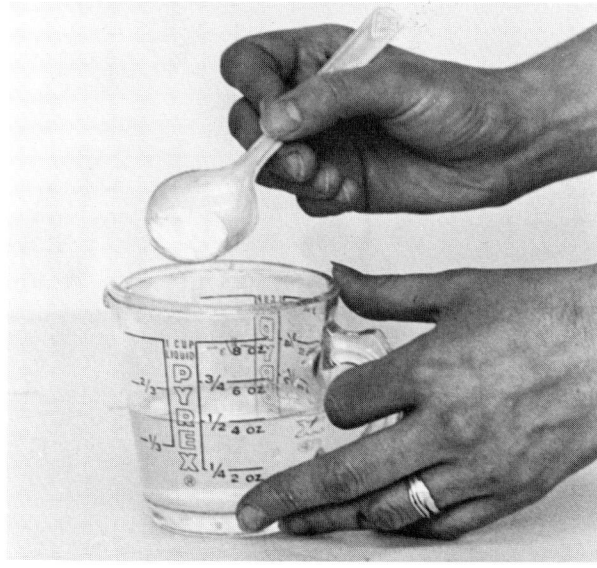

Illus. 9. When preparing the basic mordant recipe, measure carefully.

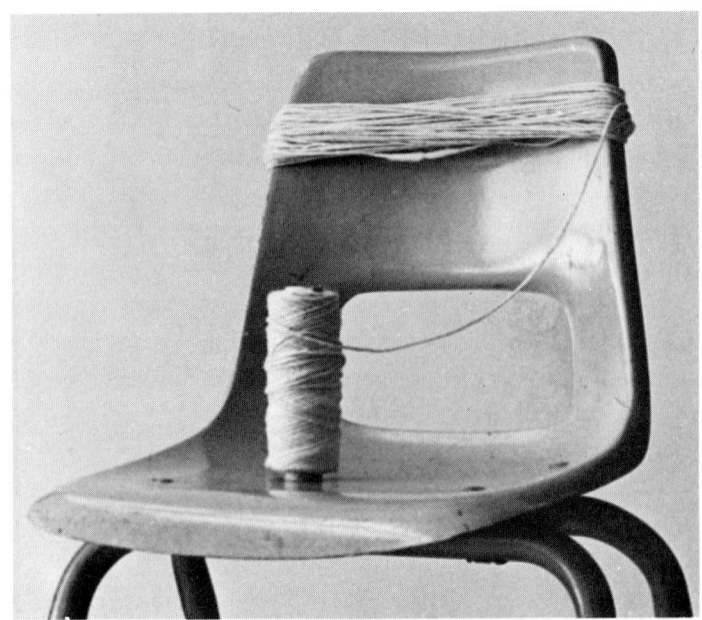

Illus. 10. To prepare your yarn for dyeing, you can skein it on a chair back . . .

Illus. 11. . . . or on your arm like this.

Preparing the Yarn

Most commercial yarn is available in 4- or 8-ounce skeins or hanks. The natural dye recipes in this book are based on one pound or 16 ounces of dry yarn. If you want to dye smaller amounts, just decrease the recipes proportionately.

Natural fibers have an affinity for natural dyes; pure wool takes natural dyes more readily than any other fiber. Synthetic fibers, such as rayon, acetate, acrylics and all blended yarns, resist the dye and, at best, the results are temporary pale tints. Cotton, linen, and silk, though natural fibers and compatible with natural dyes, require a long and complicated mordant process which is difficult even for the experienced artist-craftsman.

Use unbleached wool (cream color) if you can, because the bleaching process which makes wool white also destroys some of its basic composition, making it less durable.

Skein off the wool in a large oval so that the dye and mordant can penetrate evenly. Use a chair back or your arm for this. Don't skein the entire pound of wool in one oval. Several smaller skeins (2- to 4-ounce sizes) take the dye faster and more uniformly. Another advantage in working with smaller skeins is that if you take them out of the dye at different intervals, you can create several different shades of a color from just a single dye.

Tie off the wool in about four places with a non-shrinking white cord (cotton is good). If you use a colored cord, its dye will

Illus. 12. Tie off your wool skeins in several places to avoid tangling in the dye-bath.

Illus. 13. Work the wool in a back-and-forth motion in the dye-bath. Do not use a circular movement because it might cause tangling.

stain the wool. The tie-off should be secure enough to stop the wool from tangling in the dye, but free enough to ensure even penetration of the dye and mordant. Soak the yarn in water for about half an hour at a water temperature similar to that of the dye-bath you'll be using. The purpose of the soak is twofold: to remove air from the wool and soften it to facilitate even dye penetration; and to prevent a sudden or violent shock to the wool when it is immersed in the dye-bath, thereby preventing shrinkage and felting (matting).

Preparing the Dye-Bath

The dye liquor you have prepared is a color concentrate which must be diluted to make 4 gallons of liquid, enough to allow the wool immersed in it to move around freely, ensuring even penetration of the dye. If the dye liquor is still hot, use cold water when you dilute it, bringing it close to the temperature of the water the wool has been soaking in.

Dyeing the Wool

Submerge the wool in the dye-bath and heat to a simmer. This is a pre-boil state and if you use a thermometer, it can range from a low simmer of 170° to a high simmer of 190°F. (77° to 88°C. approximately). Hold it at a simmer for one hour, the time needed for the mordant to "take" permanently on the yarn. If some of the dye-bath evaporates, remove the yarn, replenish with hot water, and re-enter the yarn. At intervals, work the wool back and forth to encourage even penetration; a circular motion may tangle the yarn. Keep the yarn submerged in the dye at all times. If you have soaked the wool long enough, it should not float at the top of the water, but if your wool does, it helps to put a flat plate right into the water over the wool.

After the first hour, check the color of the wool. You may remove it whenever the result satisfies you. Later you will learn how to use mordants before or after dyeing to create different effects; but the advantage of mordanting and dyeing the wool in one process is that it is quicker, it puts less strain on the wool and, in the case of reds and yellows, it yields brighter colors.

With most dyes, you must allow for the fact that the color will be lighter when the wool is dry. Don't simmer the yarn for more than two hours; wool is sensitive to heat and gradually decomposes with prolonged boiling. Once the heat is turned off, however, you can leave the wool in the dye-bath as it cools. Letting it soak overnight will produce a color that may be a little deeper and richer.

Rinsing the Wool

When you remove the yarns from the dye-bath, rinse them to remove excess dye. The first rinse should be with hot water, successive rinses cooler. Continue this process until no color comes from the wool. If you have left the wool to cool in the dye-bath overnight, use cold rinses. After the wool is clean, squeeze

Illus. 14. Remove the yarn carefully from the dye-bath with a wooden stick or spoon.

it gently, wrap it in a towel to extract excess moisture, and hang it up to dry. You can drape it over a clothesline or a drying rack. Make sure that air can circulate freely around the wool. You may hang it outside to dry, but do not leave it in direct sunlight.

Be sure to rinse the wool thoroughly. Otherwise, when it dries, the dye may rub off or "crock," and when you hang it to dry, you will have added problems: the wool at the bottom of the skein will dry darker because the excess dye accumulates there. Turn the wool while it is drying; the wool will dry faster and soften a faulty rinse. As with all wool products, never use a clothes dryer. Keep the process natural.

Natural Loom—Natural Dye

Here is a decorative construction that is enhanced by using yarns that have been colored with natural dyes. Bend a long flexible branch into an inverted "U" and wire two smaller branches across it to make a loom. Run some cotton string up and down between the top and bottom horizontal branches, keeping the strands about $\frac{1}{4}$ inch apart: this is the "warp." You can cut small notches into the branches to prevent the warp from shifting on the wood (see Illus. 37).

Two simple weaves produce the final design. The first is the "tabby" weave, which you make by horizontally threading pieces of wool yarn alternately under and over the warp. The wool that moves horizontally across the warp is the "weft."

The second process, which produces a more textured finish, is the "soumak" weave. Make it by skipping over 4 warp threads and then going back under 2. This "over-4, back-2" has much the same rhythm as the sewing backstitch. A row of tabby after each row of soumak will help secure this somewhat loose weave. Make some loops by weaving a tabby and then pulling it up between the warp threads. A second row of tabby will secure the loops. Cut some of the loops to create a pile effect. Make the fringe with a series of square knots in a macramé style. Leave the final weaving permanently on the simple frame loom.

2. Exploring with Natural Dyes

Some of the most rewarding experiences with natural dyes come from capturing the color trapped in hard substances like barks and roots. You will need to spend more time collecting and preparing the dye, but the results are well worth it.

Purchasing some additional chemicals will enable you to work with other mordant recipes to obtain a wide color range from a single dye source, simply by varying the mordant. You can mordant and dye the wool in separate processes, enabling you to mordant a large amount of wool at one time, then dye it in smaller lots using a variety of dye sources. When you mordant your wool ahead of time, you can take full advantage of those fresh flower-heads or berries you just collected. Simply use the amounts of differently mordanted wool that you want to dye, and produce two or three different tones—all in the same dye-bath.

Collecting Barks and Other Hard Sources

Colors from bark or any source with a high tannin content darken and enhance with age. The colors shift, relate to one another, and reveal the very essence and charm of natural dyes. Nature always dictates the color—the health of the plant, its location, its age, the quality of the soil, and the season all affect the strength of the dye and create slight color variations. Choose healthy-looking sources: wood and twigs are strongest in the spring and the autumn when the sap is most active. If you are collecting in any other season, gather more dyestuff than is

Illus. 15. Hard dye sources include barks and roots.

Illus. 16. When removing twigs and branches, be sure to protect the tree from injury by pruning it properly.

called for in the recipe. Collect the dyematter in large sacks or paper bags; bring along pruners and a penknife. Gardening gloves help prevent blisters.

In order to protect the health of a tree, prune it correctly. Use entire twigs that are at least 2 years old; younger shoots have less dye content. Use sharp, clean pruners. Make the cut slightly above the trunk or stem that the branch grows out of. Take along "tree wound paint" to seal the exposed area. Never peel the bark away from the entire circumference of a living tree; this would kill it. It is far better to collect bark from recently felled trees. When you fill a large grocery bag, you have enough material to dye one pound of wool.

Collecting Roots

Generally, roots and tree bark yield similar colors. Roots of most plants are the strongest in the autumn when the plant is preparing to store its winter supply of food. Bring along a shovel and an axe for tree and shrub roots. With such sources as the dandelion, you will have to uproot the entire plant, but with tree and shrub roots, dig out only one or two sections, so you do not cause permanent injury to any one plant. You can take roots from several plants of the same species, if you need additional dyestuff.

Collecting Cones and Hulls

Cones should be picked when they are open and without sap. Sap clings to the wool and affects the dye process.

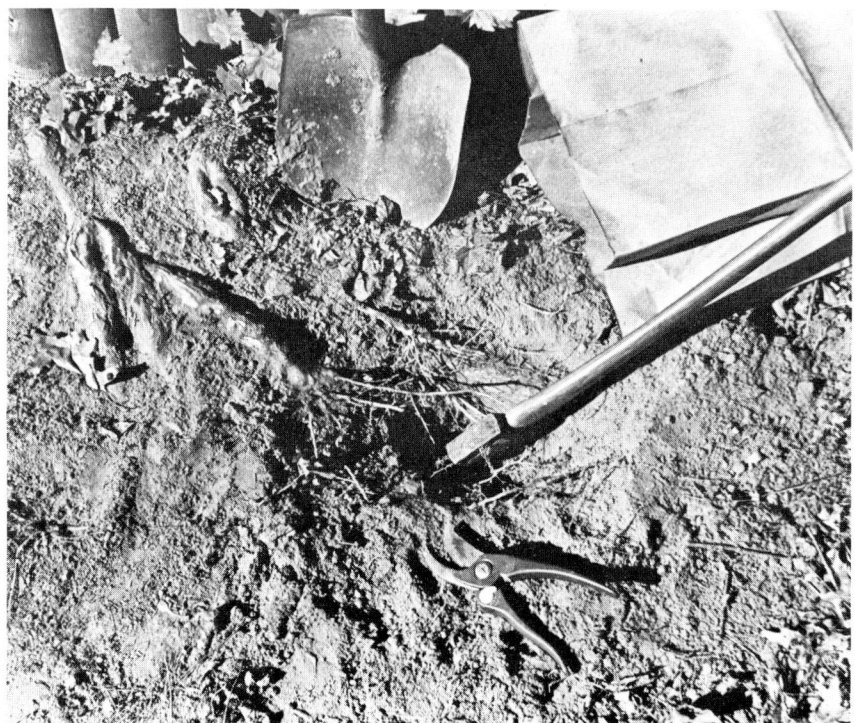

Illus. 17. Dig around and cut only one or two pieces of a tree root to avoid harm to the tree.

Illus. 18. Cones, hulls, and gum balls all yield color.

Hulls are strongest when they are still green, but you may use them when they turn brown.

You don't have to limit yourself to these sources; any root,

Illus. 19. Sweet gum balls will produce tan to grey dye colors.

bark, hull, or cone yields color. Collect whatever is convenient for you and follow the corresponding recipe. When you set out to find a particular source, you will look more attentively at everything. Notice how closely the colors in nature relate to the soft hues you get from natural dyes. For any of these sources you need one peck or 8 dry quarts to produce enough dye for one pound of wool.

Color	Source
Yellow, Orange, Tan	Apple tree bark and twigs
Rose-tan to Brown	Willow bark and twigs
Tans to Brown	Dandelion roots
	Black walnut hulls
	Pine cones (all species)
Browns	Alder bark and twigs
	Hickory nut hulls
Tan to grey	Sweet gum balls

Preparing the Dye

Chop twigs into 3-inch pieces approximately, exposing as many plant cells as possible, even skinning the outer bark from

Illus. 20. Twigs and small branches should be chopped into pieces so as to expose as much as possible of the inner plant.

Illus. 21. Bruise cones and sweet gum balls with a hammer.

the twig. Large bark pieces and roots should be chopped too, after they have been washed. Bruise cones and sweet gum balls with a hammer.

When the dyestuff is ready, cover it with water and soak it overnight. The next day, boil it from 2 to 4 hours, or until the water appears to have absorbed all the dye. If the water evaporates, replenish it with hot water. Strain away the pulp and increase the dye to equal 4 gallons. The dye is now ready to accept the wool.

Water

What type of water do you have in your area? Is it acid or alkaline? When you work with natural dyes, it is best to use neutral water, and if water from your tap is not "right," you can correct it easily. The best way to determine the exact

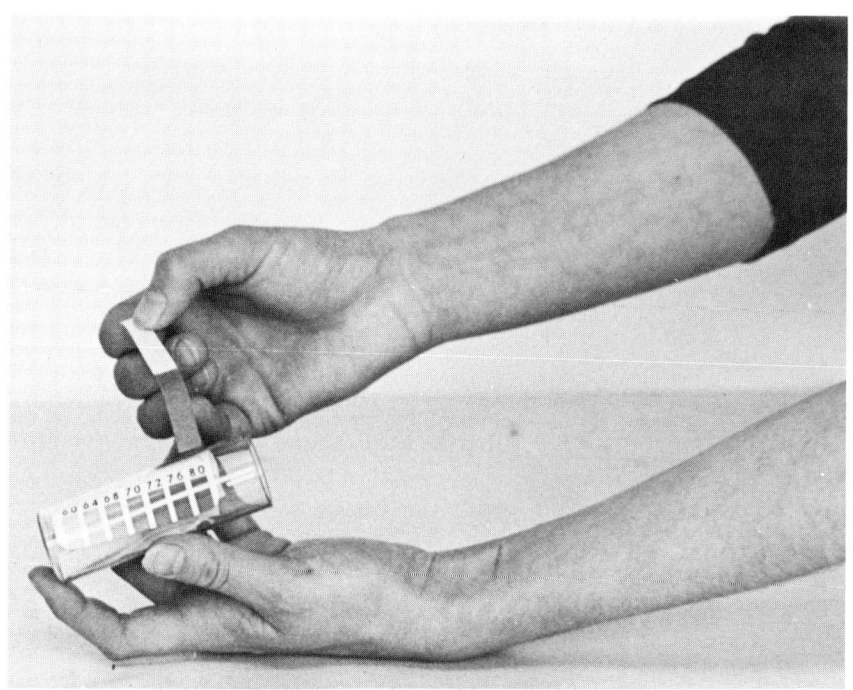

Illus. 22. The water you use should be neutral—neither acid nor alkaline. Indicator paper will help you determine the nature of your water.

properties of water is to use indicator paper. Fill an enamel pot with water, dip the paper into the water and then compare its color to the color chart on the indicator package. The chart range is from 6.0 (acid) to 8.0 (alkaline); neutral is 7.0. If the color of the indicator paper corresponds to 7.0, the water is neutral. If it indicates that your water supply is acidic, add baking soda or borax until the reading reaches neutral. Usually just a small amount—a teaspoonful or less—will neutralize the water. If your water supply is alkaline (sometimes referred to as "base"), add some clear vinegar until the reading reaches neutral. Use a new strip of paper each time you need to test water.

Litmus paper works the same way with a difference in the range. Indicator paper runs from 6.0 to 8.0; litmus papers from 0 to 14; 7 is neutral on both. Most pet shops carry these products for testing aquarium water; all chemical supply houses carry both types of paper.

The next question is whether the water is hard or soft. If you use hard water with natural dyes, the high mineral content may streak your yarn and cause irregular distribution of the dye on the wool. Soft water has a low mineral content and is far better to use for dyeing. If you are not sure about the mineral content of the water, test it by washing your hands with soap. Soap tends to linger with soft water and rinse off immediately with hard water. Pet shops also carry products to test water for mineral content.

You can soften hard water by adding any commercial water softener that you can buy in a grocery. Add the softener before you test it with indicator or litmus paper, because the softener may affect the pH factor (the measure of acidity or alkalinity) of the water.

Mordanting the Wool

You can mordant wool long before you are ready to dye it. The mordant becomes fixed on the wool; it prepares the wool to absorb color and it makes the dye fast. Even when the wool is dyed much later, a chemical union takes place between the mordant which is already in the wool and the dye. Besides alum and tartar, which produce the softest tones most like the dyebath itself, there are three other commonly used mordants:

Chrome (potassium dichromate)—which gives slightly darker or brassier results than alum.

Tin (stannous chloride)—which gives the brightest results.

Iron (ferrous sulphate)—which gives the darkest results.

These mordants are most readily available from chemical supply houses (see list of suppliers on page 90). They range in purity—and price. For natural dyeing, the technical grade (least expensive) works fine. Buy the mordants in powder or granular form if you can; if you buy crystals, you must hammer them into a powder yourself. Store them in a dry place and use them very carefully; many are poisonous if taken internally; some give off unpleasant but harmless fumes. Using various mordants you may obtain several values of a color or produce an entirely

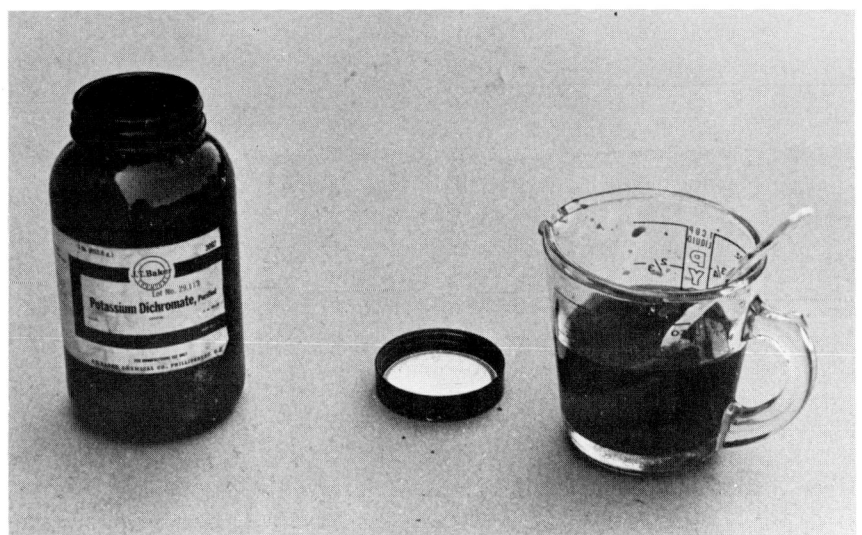

Illus. 23. Potassium dichromate is a common mordant, used to produce darker or brassier tones than does alum.

different color from the same dye. Take the onion recipe as an example. With alum and tartar as the mordant, you can expect a soft yellow. If you use a chrome mordant, you'll get a mustard color or ochre. A tin mordant should produce yellow-orange; iron, a deep tan. By varying the mordants you use, you can create an array of colors from just one source.

These mordant recipes are planned for one pound of wool, the amount you'll need for most projects. However, you may skein off the wool into smaller hanks (2- or 4-ounce sizes), which equal one pound altogether, and mordant them at one time. Later you can use them in combination with differently mordanted skeins to produce a variety of shades and colors from a single dye-bath. Using wool that has been mordanted in advance, you can dye less than one pound of it at a time which means that you won't need as much dyestuff. Cut down the quantities of dyestuff proportionately as you cut down the amount of wool, but be sure to follow the instructions carefully. If you don't mordant the wool long enough, or if you use too little mordant, the dye may later crock.

Mordant Recipes for One Pound of Wool
Chrome (potassium dichromate) Mordant
$\frac{1}{4}$ ounce chrome

4 gallons neutral water

Tie off the wool and soak it in warm water. Dissolve the chrome in $\frac{1}{2}$ cup of warm water (mineral salts dissolve faster in warm water). When the chemical is fully dissolved, pour the solution into the 4 gallons of water. Stir. This is the mordant bath. Heat it and, when it is warm, immerse the wool. Cover the pot and slowly raise the temperature to a simmer. Hold the bath at that point for one hour. Check from time to time to see that the wool is fully submerged or the mordanting will be uneven and cause streaks in the dye color. After the first hour, turn off the heat and let the wool cool in the mordant (overnight if you wish) until it can be handled. The wool will have an ochre tint. Gently squeeze out the excess moisture, rinse, and store the wool in a dark place until you are ready to use it.

Some dyers add $\frac{1}{2}$ ounce of cream of tartar to this mordant recipe to soften the wool and brighten the eventual color, but the difference is rarely discernible.

When this wool is exposed to the oxygen in the air, the chrome mordant on it produces a color change called "oxidation." The wool will reflect an umber-greenish tint. If this happens, the oxidized wool, when you dye it, will take on a slightly different color from unoxidized wool. If you want to prevent oxidation, wrap the wool in a towel and store it in a plastic bag or dark place. If only parts of the skein oxidize, the wool will dye unevenly. Your only choice then is to expose the entire skein to light so that it will oxidize completely.

Some dyers prefer to use chrome-mordanted wool immediately, and age their alum wool for several days. But because the mordant is fixed permanently on the yarn, either of these mordanted wools may be used immediately or kept for a length of time before dyeing. If you choose to store the wool, make sure it is dry or mildew will set in. Iron-mordanted wool will also oxidize, turning a light rust color if you leave it exposed to light. Too much chrome causes the wool to resist the dye.

Tin (stannous chloride) Mordant
$\frac{1}{2}$ ounce tin
2 ounces cream of tartar
$\frac{3}{4}$ ounce oxalic acid
4 gallons neutral water

Tie off the wool and soak it in warm water. Dissolve the mordant ingredients separately, each in $\frac{1}{2}$ cup of warm water, and add them to the 4 gallons. Stir after each ingredient is added. Warm the mordant bath and immerse the wool. Cover. Bring the water to a simmer and hold at that heat for one hour. Work the wool now and then and make sure it is fully submerged. After the first hour, turn off the heat, leaving the wool in the mordant bath until you can handle it. The wool will develop a yellow tint. Squeeze out the excess moisture, then rinse the wool with some mild soap. Rinse it again until the water is clear of soap, and store the wool until you are ready to use it. The soap bath helps offset the hardening effect of the tin.

Tin is the most difficult mordant to use. Too much tin makes the wool brittle, and after several years it will fray. Measure the mordant carefully.

Iron (ferrous sulphate) Mordant
$\frac{3}{4}$ ounce granular ferrous sulphate
$\frac{3}{4}$ ounce oxalic acid
4 gallons neutral water

Tie off the wool and soak it in warm water. Dissolve the iron in $\frac{1}{2}$ cup of warm water, and add it to 4 gallons of water in the mordant pot. Dissolve the oxalic acid separately in $\frac{1}{2}$ cup of warm water, then add it to the mordant pot. Stir, enter the wool, cover, and bring the bath to a simmer. Hold at that point for one hour. With this mordant the wool will turn a warm cream color. Let the wool cool, rinse, and then store the wool until you are ready to use it.

Too much iron will "take" unevenly and make the wool streak when you dye it; eventually the wool will disintegrate. Iron is not strong enough to use alone as a mordant. Without the oxalic acid, the dye color fades when exposed to light.

Basic Mordant Procedure
Here is a quick checklist of the steps common to all mordanting procedures.
 1. Tie off and soak the wool.
 2. Measure the mordant chemicals carefully, dissolve them completely in a separate ½ cup of warm water, and add them one at a time to the dye-bath.
 3. The mordant bath is 4 gallons of water which should be neutral before you add the mordants. All mordants are alkaline, except chrome, which is slightly acid.
 4. Enter the yarns, increase the temperature slowly, and simmer according to the recipe—generally one hour.
 5. Cover the pot to contain odor and prevent oxidation of the wool.
 6. Make sure the yarn is completely submerged at all times, to ensure even mordanting. Occasionally work the wool for even penetration. A flat plate placed on top of the wool right in the bath helps keep the wool submerged in the bath.
 7. Leave the yarn in the mordant bath while it cools enough for you to handle it; many dyers leave it to cool overnight. Rinse the wool and let it dry. You can use the wool right away or store it for future projects.

Labels
It is frustrating to try to duplicate a color when you don't know exactly which mordant produced it. It is useful therefore to use some method of marking your wool to indicate the mordant you used. Many dyers use a knot system to indicate the mordant; others use tags to record both the mordant and the dye source.

With the knot system, tie the knots at one end of each strand of the yarn or in the tie-off cords. Tie one knot for alum, two for chrome and so forth, but be sure to keep a record of what each knot means!

With the tag system, attach a label to the wool to be used like the tag of a tea bag. Tie a length of string to one end of the wool skein and attach a small paper tag to the other end of it. A 12-inch string is about right, because long cords get tangled

Illus. 24. The knot system for labelling the mordants used. Tie one knot for alum.

while short ones are not long enough to hang outside the mordant pot. Use a durable paper such as cardboard or tag-

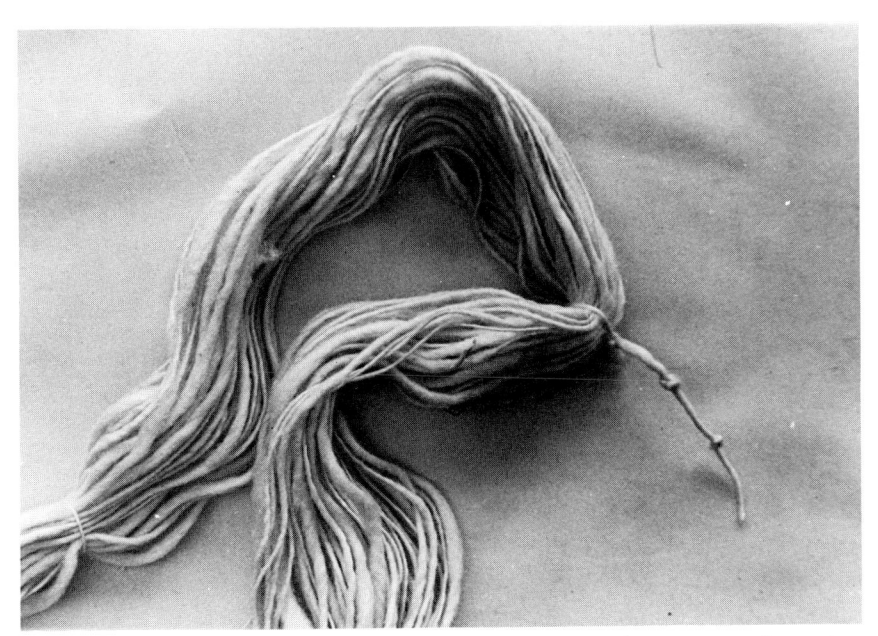

Illus. 25. Two knots indicate chrome was used as a mordant for this wool.

Illus. 26. A natural-dyed finger-woven project in a natural setting.

Illus. 27. The hand-woven purse seems to blend right into its out-of-doors setting.

Illus. 28. Here is a sample of some of the colors you can achieve when you use natural dyes.

Illus. 29. The colors in this hooked rug came from cochineal, logwood, sweet gum balls, and rhododendron leaves.

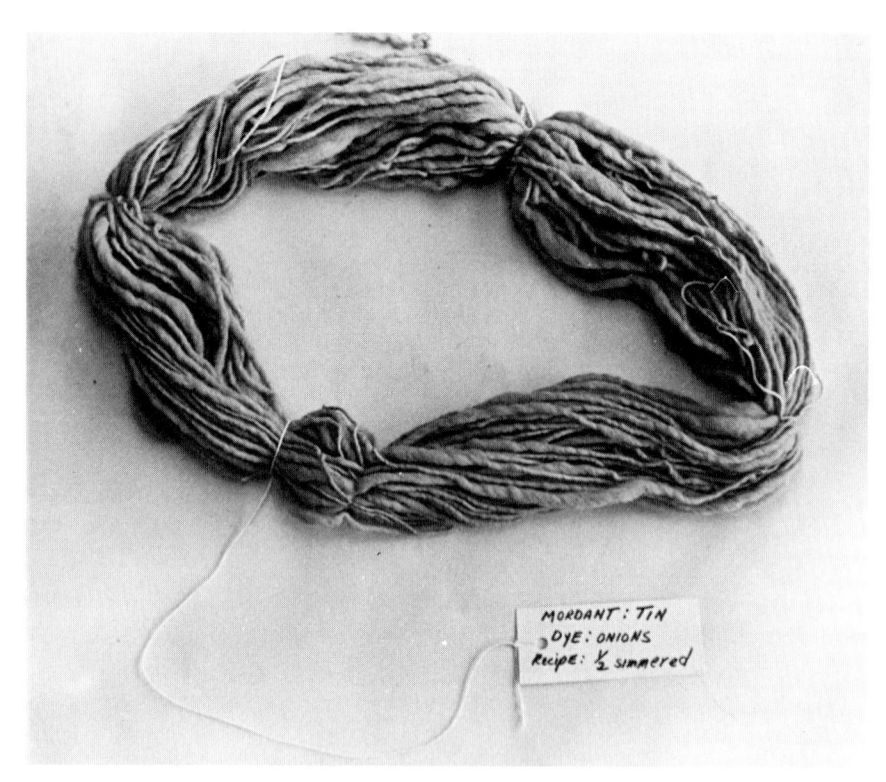

Illus. 30. If you use the tag system for recording your dyed yarns, cite the mordant, the dye, and the recipe.

board, since even with long cords, tags sometimes get wet. On the tag, record the mordant, the dye source, a brief description of the dye recipe, and the batch number.

Dyeing Already-Mordanted Wool

Add cold water to the dye liquor (sometimes referred to as "ooze") to increase it to 4 gallons. Warm the dye-bath and immerse the wet, already-mordanted wool. Bring the bath to a simmer and hold it at that point until the wool has absorbed as much dye as it can. Dyeing time usually varies from 30 to 60 minutes. You may cover the pot. Do not crowd the wool by dyeing more than one pound at a time. The wool must always be able to move freely to ensure even penetration of the dye. When the color pleases you, remove the wool, rinse, and dry.

Batches

A dye-bath is depleted when the liquid is clear, or "spent." Before it is spent, it may yield several batches of color, each batch, however, lighter than the preceding one. These progressive batches work wonderfully when you want to blend wools in a project. Label them: Batch I, Batch II, and so on. If you need more wool of a particular shade, you will have a better chance of re-creating it by repeating the same sequence.

Tints

Wool absorbs dye until it becomes saturated. If the dye-bath is weak, you will have to let the yarn cook for a longer time and it still may not absorb as much dye as it is capable of accepting. The result may be only a tint of the color you want. While tints may be attractive, all that extra heat puts a strain on the wool, and there is no reason to overwork it in a weak bath.

Some dyers produce tints by soaking the wool in a cool dye-bath. This is a slower process, but for light colors the wool should be dyed more slowly, so it can absorb the color throughout its grist (thickness), without becoming dark on the outside while remaining light on the inside. This is a particularly important point to remember for "cut" projects, such as pile rugs. If you soak the wool first in hot water for at least half an hour, you can try producing tints by dipping the wool into a hot dye-bath.

Judging the Results

If your first results are indifferent or bland, don't be discouraged. Those pale colors are often the most valuable when you want to create blends, color shifts, or pattern changes. Dyed wool often looks different in a finished product than it does in a skein. Remember that you cannot use too much dyestuff when you prepare a dye. Stronger dyes cut down on dyeing time and are strong enough to give successive batches.

Hooked Rug

To hook a rug, you need only some backing (burlap, hessian or monk's cloth), a rug hooker (either the punch or latch style), and dyed wool. You can use sweater wool, but rug wool is

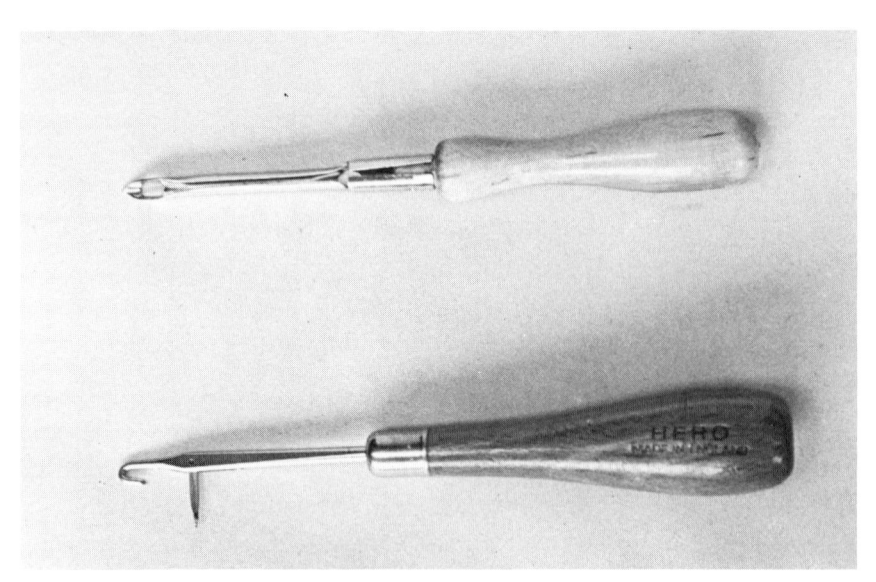

Illus. 31. You can use either a punch-type or a latch-type rug hooker.

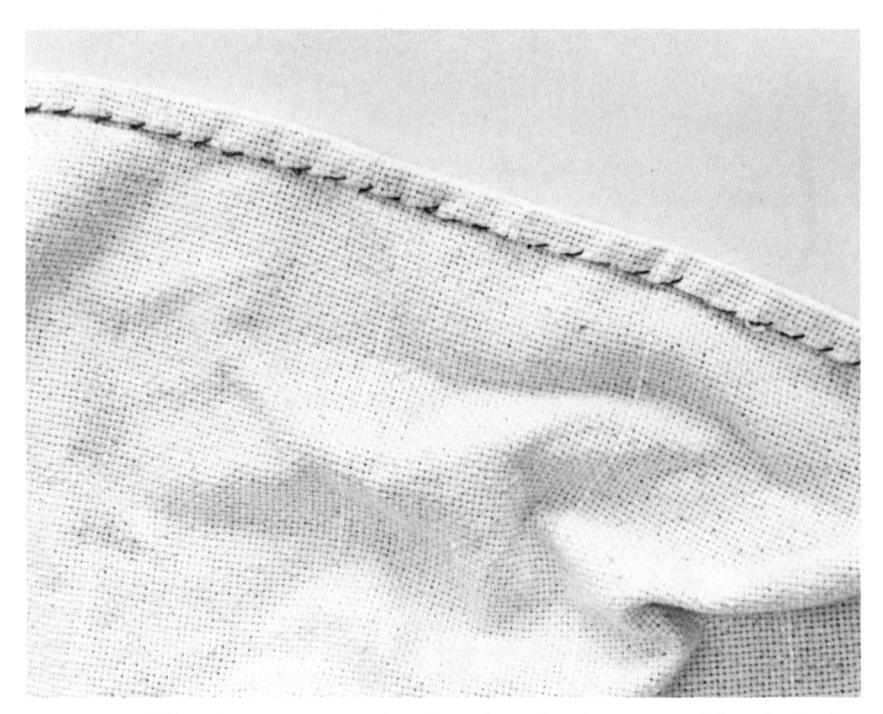

Illus. 32. Whether you use burlap (hessian) or monk's cloth for your backing, be sure to hem it to prevent the edges from fraying.

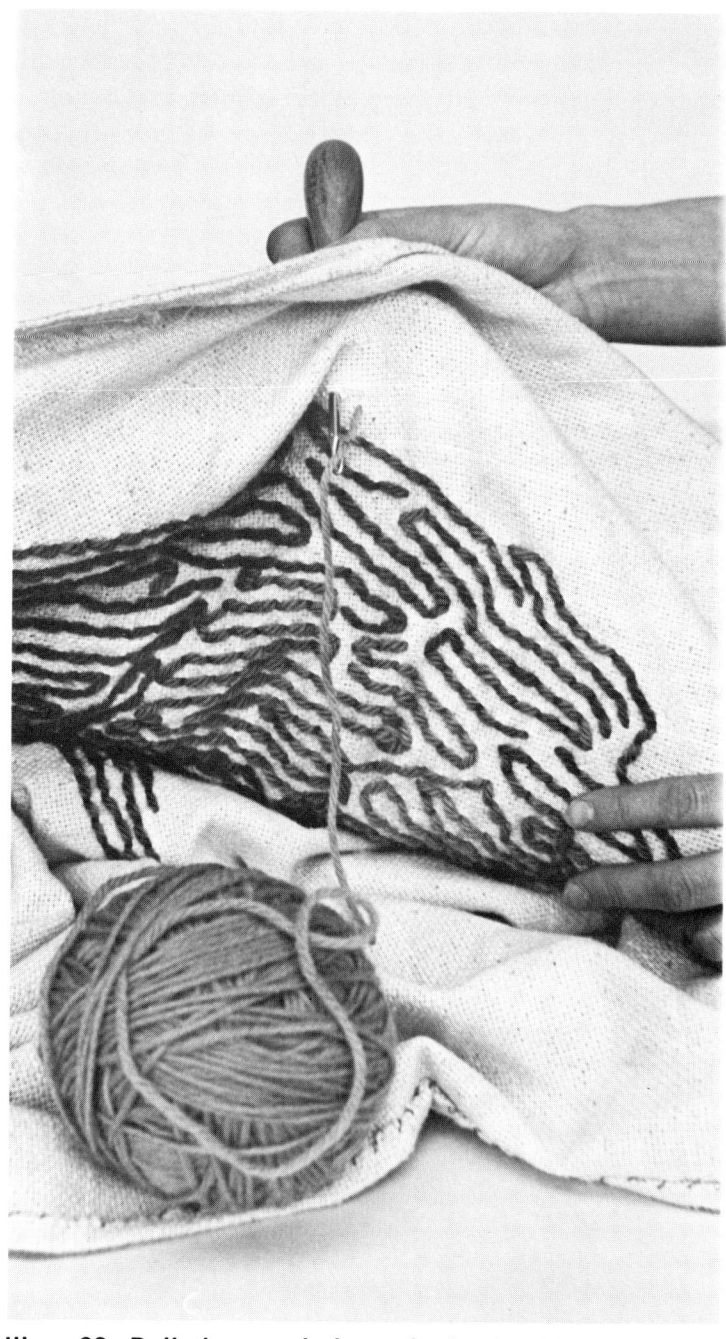

Illus. 33. Pull the wool through the backing with the hooker.

coarser and wears better. (See list of suppliers.) Rugs do not have to be rectangular or square; you can cut the backing into any shape. To prevent fraying, hem the backing before you hook the rug. Then with the hooker, pull the wool through the backing. If you are using a punch-style hooker, you work on the back or underside of the rug; a latch hooker allows you to work on the top of the rug. This is useful if you want to create a planned design.

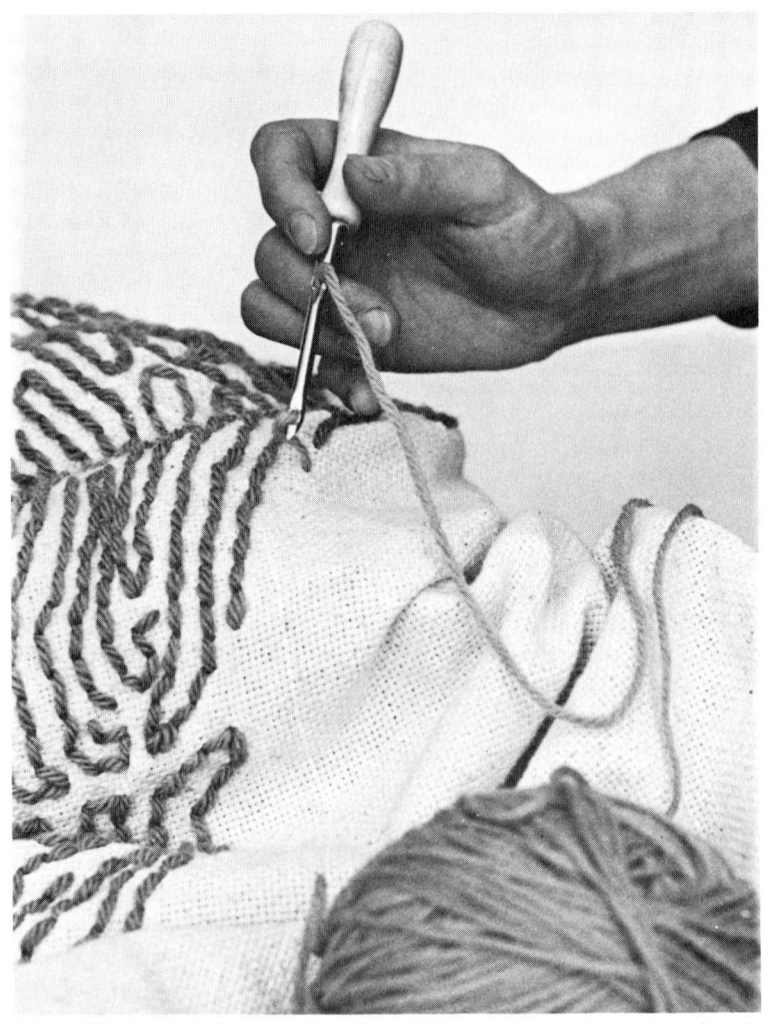

Illus. 34. A punch-type hooker lets you work on the back of the rug.

Illus. 35. If you wish, you can cut the yarn loops in your hooked rug. However, cut on an angle so that the pile stands upright.

Different pile heights produce different effects. Yarn may be left in loops or cut. Cut yarn reflects the light differently than loops and produces interesting effects. Cut pile is also sturdier than uncut; a loop may catch on a shoe and pull out a section of the rug. If you cut the loops on an angle, rather than evenly, it helps the pile stand upright for a longer time. The shorter fibers support the longer ones, maintaining a freshly vacuumed look.

Illus. 36. This hanging is made from apple bark-dyed yarns.

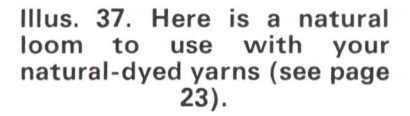

Illus. 37. Here is a natural loom to use with your natural-dyed yarns (see page 23).

Illus. 38. Close-up of natural-dyed yarns.

3. Experiments with Natural Dyes

Take a look at the plant life around you. The real excitement of natural dyes comes when you leave recipes behind and start creating your own. If you happen on some lichens or black walnut hulls, you can use them without any mordant and the color will be permanent. These are called "substantive" sources and they are a good quick way of getting permanent colors without the expense or bother of mordants.

Most dyes, however, are "adjective," and you need to use a

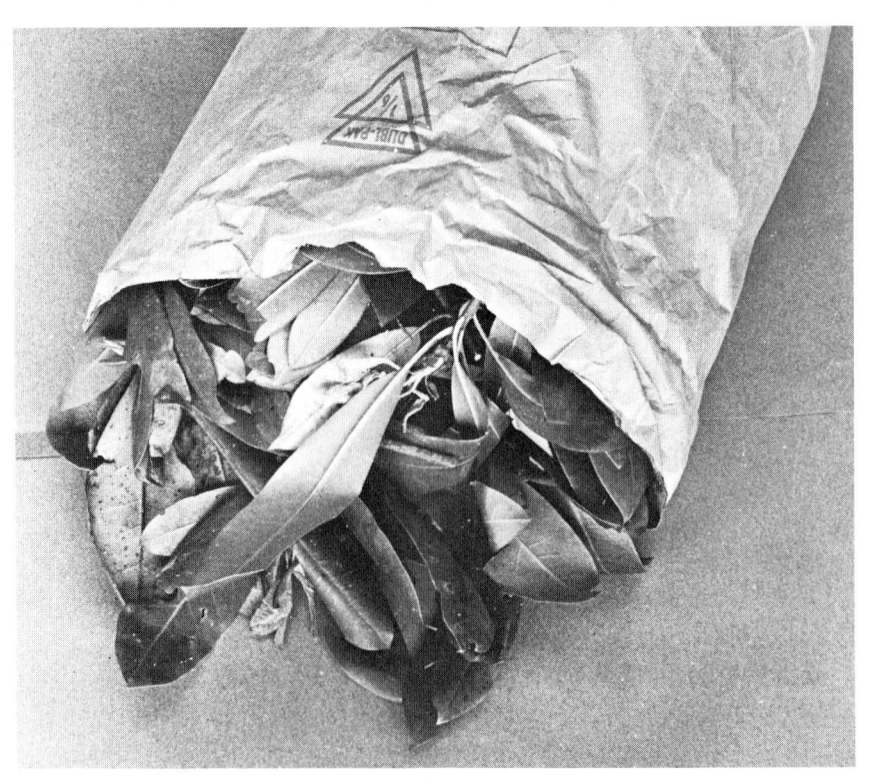

Illus. 39. Rhododendron leaves are "adjective" sources, which means you must use a mordant to obtain a permanent dye from them.

mordant to make the color permanent. Onion peels, rhododendron leaves, and most plant life fall into this class. Don't be fooled by so-called "fugitive" sources. These sometimes produce appealing colors, but they fade quickly even when you use mordants. The spice tumeric, beet roots, blueberries, apple peels, and certain other fruits fall into this category. Flowerheads vary: dyes made from rose petals fade; those from marigolds don't. It is an adventure discovering new dyes that give reliable results.

On the next two pages, you will find 40 samples of natural-dyed yarns. Below is a description of the recipes for each one.

1. Bamboo Twigs and Leaves: Alum
2. Marigold Flower-heads: Tin
3. Onion Peels: Tin
4. Onion Peels: Chrome
5. Queen Anne's Lace Flower-heads: Alum
6. Bamboo Twigs and Leaves—Indigo Dip: Alum
7. Onion Peels-Indigo Dip: Tin
8. Onion Peels-Indigo Dip: Tin
9. Yellow Onion Peels: Alum
10. Madder Roots: Alum
11. Madder Roots: Tin
12. Madder Roots: Alum
13. Cochineal-Indigo Dip: Chrome
14. Indigo-Cochineal Dip: Chrome
15. Indigo: Chrome
16. Indigo: Iron
17. Rhododendron Leaves: Tin
18. Tea: Alum
19. Tea: Tin
20. Rhododendron Leaves: Iron
21. Logwood: Tin
22. Cochineal: Iron
23. Cochineal-Indigo Dip: Iron
24. Cochineal-Indigo Dip: Tin
25. Logwood: Chrome
26. Sumac Berry Stalk: Chrome
27. Cutch (2 Day Recipe)
28. Black Walnut Hulls: Iron
29. Pokeberries: Vinegar
30. Onion Peels-Cochineal Dip: Tin
31. Cochineal: Alum-Vinegar
32. Cochineal: Chrome
33. Onion Peels-Indigo Dip: Tin
34. Onion Peels-Indigo Dip: Chrome
35. Onion Peels-Indigo Dip: Iron
36. Onion Peels-Indigo Dip: Tin
37. Peanut Shells: Iron
38. Logwood: Alum
39. Madder Roots: Chrome
40. Cochineal: Tin

Notice that No. 7 and No. 8 have the same recipe. However, No. 8 was left in the dye a longer time. No. 10 and No. 12 also have the same recipe. No. 10 is a tight, 4-ply wool making it more difficult for the dye to permeate the tighter wool. No. 12 is 1-ply yarn. Here the looser wool takes the dye better, accounting for the darker color.

1 2 3 4

9 10 11 12

17 18 19 20

25 26 27 28

33 34 35 36

Illus. 40. See page 49 for the descriptions of the natural-dyed yarns on these two pages.

5	6	7	8
13	14	15	16
21	22	23	24
29	30	31	32
37	38	39	40

Illus. 41. To check on whether your dyed wool will fade, place a strand in a container with half of it hanging out and exposed to the sun. Comparing the two portions a few weeks later will tell you if the color is fast.

Fade Test

Run a fade test to see whether light affects your color. It's a simple process and a good idea when you are doing experimental work. Cut a length of the dyed wool; place half of it in an opaque container, such as a covered can, and leave the other half exposed to the light. Tag each test yarn, recording the dye source, the mordant, and the date the test began. Place the container in a sunny window. Fugitive color fades within about 3 weeks. Fast color shows little or no change after even 9 weeks. In some cases, of course, you might like the changed color better than the original! Natural dyes often produce pleasant surprises.

Wash Test

You should ordinarily have items made of wool dry-cleaned, but if you plan to wash a product, run a wash test. Simply wash a sample several times with soap and water and compare it to the unwashed wool.

Selecting and Storing Dyestuff

Some recipes call for a plant to be used in its entirety; others suggest you use just the leaves, or both the leaves and stalks to produce a certain color. There are many ways to use a dye source (see page 80 for a few suggestions). If a recipe calls for only flower-heads, but you use the entire plant, the result will be contaminated by the color extracted from the leaves and stalk, and you will produce a different color. This does not mean the color is wrong; it only means it is different. You may find more interesting colors by *not* following the rules! Recipes are guide-

Illus. 42. You can dry out and store your plant source material on a screen raised above the ground.

Illus. 43. Another method of drying and storing plants is to tie them in bunches and hang them in a dry place.

lines which tell you how someone else succeeded in achieving a particular color. Color is an individual experience, and working with something as flexible and variable as natural dyes always provides a chance of new and beautiful discoveries. Experiment —don't be afraid to go far afield!

Some dyers mix different plants together to get a color, as country people did a few centuries ago in their recipes for black. If you try it, keep an accurate record of the plants you use although the chances are you will not be able to produce exactly the same shade again. Black is easy to reproduce since it is the presence of all colors; but it is no easy task to repeat any other color from a combination-dye. You are dealing with materials that are always changing, and you may occasionally get wonderful but one-time results.

Many dyers gather seasonal plants and store them whole or in parts, to use as needed. If you do this, tie small clusters of entire plants with cord, and hang them in a dry, airy place. If you choose to separate the parts first, place them on a screen raised slightly above the ground, so that air can circulate around them. Turn the dyestuff from time to time to hasten the drying process. When the parts are dry, leave them on the screen, or store them in any porous bag; burlap, mesh or paper bags are fine.

These methods work best with stalks, leaves, hulls, and flower-heads. Fruits and berries may be dried or frozen. Little

Illus. 44. This fashionable hat was made from natural-dyed wool.

55

color change occurs when you freeze dyestuff; a far greater change takes place when you dry it. Use whatever method is most convenient. Not all plants can be stored; some must be used fresh. Dandelion and goldenrod, for example, will go to seed a few days after they are picked. Many plants (this is especially true of flowers) give bright colors when fresh, and darker or even different colors when dry.

Preserving Dyes

Just like vegetables or other foods, natural dyes spoil after a few days; that is why they are usually used at once, right after they are made. If you need to keep a dye for a few days, refrigerate it. If you need to keep it for more than a week, freeze it or add some sodium benzoate. This is a preservative which you can purchase at any pharmacy. A dye may last for months if you add one teaspoon of sodium benzoate per gallon of dye, and then store it in large, air-tight containers.

If a dye smells unpleasant after you have kept it for a time, don't use it. If a mould forms over the top, but it smells all right, just skim it off and use the dye.

The After-Mordants

Besides the basic mordant recipes, there are some other ways to control your final colors. You may brighten a color, darken it, or bring out the "green" in it by using after-mordants.

All the following recipes are based on one pound of wool. If you are using less than one pound, reduce the quantities proportionately. For small amounts, estimate, as Grandma did, with a pinch of the mineral salts. When you use after-mordants, it is better to underestimate and then add more if needed.

Blooming

If the resulting color is not bright enough to suit you when it is time to remove the yarn from the dye-bath, lift the wool out and dissolve $\frac{1}{2}$ ounce of stannous chloride in warm water; then stir it into the dye-bath. Re-enter the yarn and simmer. This process is called "blooming," and while it will not change the color, it will brighten it. Use a soap bath followed by a clear rinse after blooming.

Saddening

If the color is not dark enough, remove the yarn and add $\frac{1}{2}$ ounce of dissolved ferrous sulphate to the dye-bath. Return the yarn and simmer until the shade is right. This process is called "saddening."

Greening

If you would like to bring out the green tones in a color, remove the yarn and add one to two ounces of copper sulphate to the dye-bath. Return the yarn and simmer until you reach a color you like. Copper sulphate works well with onion peels or any yellow dye. Some dyers use two ounces of copper sulphate as a regular mordant for one pound of wool, but it works best as an after-mordant.

You may also bloom, sadden, or green your colors in separate processes, rather than in the original dye-bath which you may want to use for additional wool. In this case, just add the after-mordant chemical to 4 gallons of hot water and immerse the dyed wool until you get the color you want.

Glauber's Salt

If you are especially particular about even color distribution, try adding Glauber's salt (hydrated sodium sulphate) to the dye-bath. When the water is saturated with Glauber's salt, it absorbs the dye more slowly, and the wool in turn absorbs the dye more slowly and uniformly. The dye also becomes more permanent.

Glauber's salt is actually an old-fashioned laxative still carried by some pharmacies and all chemical supply houses. To use it in a dye-bath, start about midpoint in the dyeing process. Remove the partially dyed wool, add $\frac{1}{2}$ cup of Glauber's salt to the dye-bath, and stir until fully dissolved. The salt tends to dull the color, but you can overcome that effect somewhat by adding $\frac{1}{4}$ cup of cream of tartar. Re-enter the yarn and complete the dyeing process.

Glauber's salt works particularly well with dark colors. You can also use it if you dyed the wool without it and find the results uneven. In this case, dissolve one cup of the salt for every pound of wool, either in the dye itself or in a pot of hot

Illus. 45. The varied shades and colors of these yarns were derived from American birch leaves and lichen.

Illus. 46 (opposite). All of these colors come from carrot tops, but different mordants and after-mordants were used. 1. Tin—no after-mordant. 2. Alum—bloomed. 3. Alum—no after-mordant. 4. Chrome—no after-mordant. 5. Chrome—bloomed. 6. Alum—greened. 7. Tin—greened. 8. Chrome—greened. 9. Iron—greened. 10. Alum—saddened. 11. Chrome—saddened. 12. Iron—no after-mordant. Remember, do not bloom or sadden tin- or iron-mordanted wool. Blooming would only add more tin to the already tin-mordanted wool, an unnecessary step, and would add brightening to the iron-mordanted wool, where presumably you are trying for dark results. If you sadden tin-mordanted wool, you would darken the naturally bright results you were trying for when you mordanted the wool. Saddening iron-mordanted wool would do nothing more than add more iron. (See pages 56 and 57.)

1	2	3
4	5	6
7	8	9
10	11	12

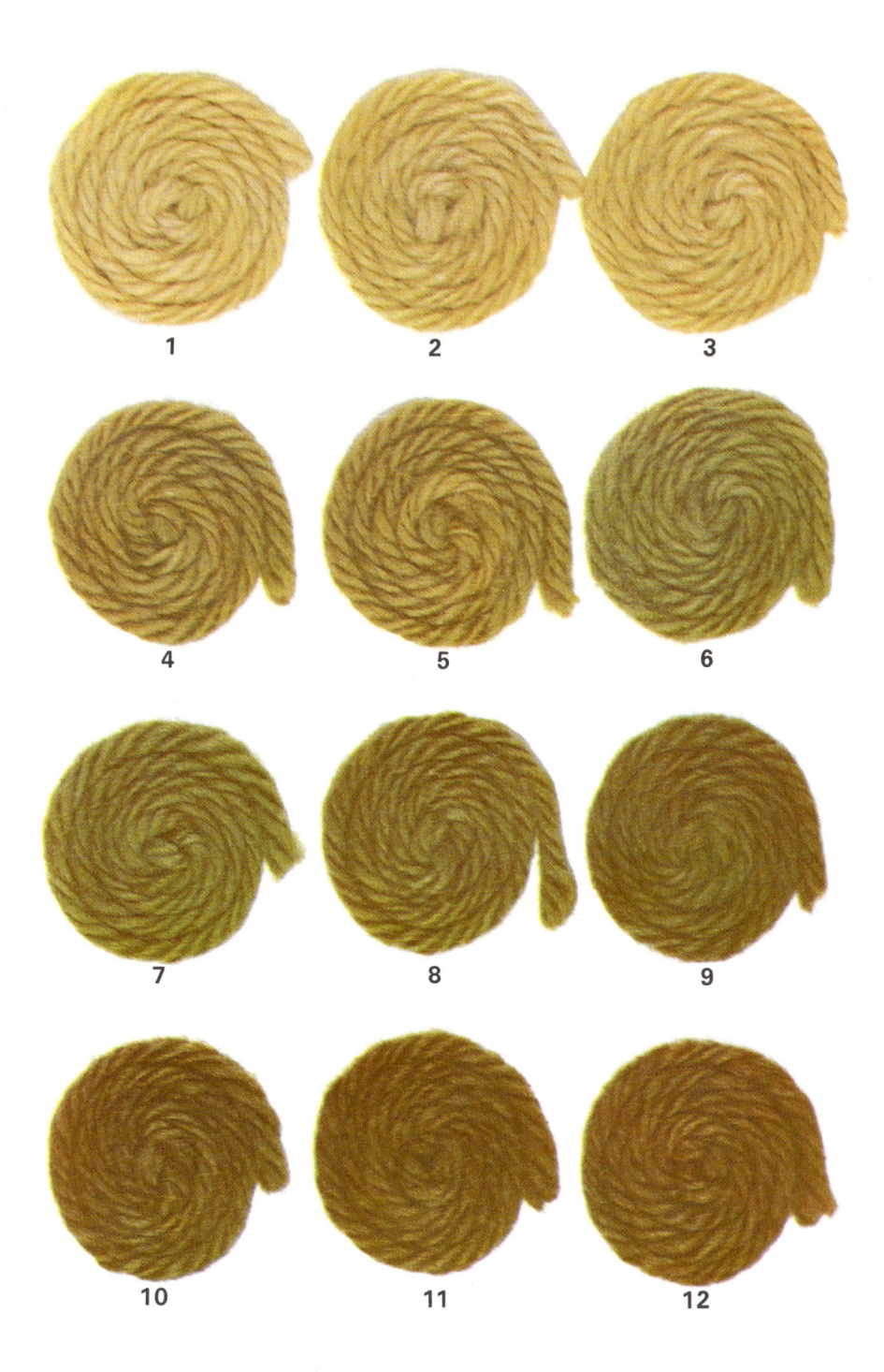

water. Add the wet wool and simmer for about half an hour or until the color grows more even.

Glauber's salt is not a cure-all for problem dyeing. It does lengthen the process, darken and dull color, but cannot salvage a badly streaked hank of yarn.

To Set Dyes with Tannin Content

Dyes with a tannin content tend to darken with age. If you want to set a color obtained from a tannin dye, use an after-mordant.

If the first mordant you used was alum, make a separate after-mordant bath by adding one teaspoon of chrome to 4 gallons of hot water. Let the chrome dissolve. Add ½ cup of vinegar, then stir the solution. Immerse the wool immediately after dyeing and simmer for 15 minutes.

If the first mordant you used was tin, add one tablespoon of hydrochloric acid to the original dye-bath. Use it carefully, because, even in a weak solution, this is a fairly strong acid and can burn your skin if it touches it. Buy a concentration of 0.1 molar from a chemical supplier; this strength will set the color. Always add the acid directly to the 4 gallons of water, and use a plastic, not metal, spoon for measuring. Clean it immediately after use.

If the first mordant was chrome, add ½ teaspoon of copper sulphate and ½ cup of vinegar to the original dye-bath.

If the first mordant was iron, adding ½ cup of vinegar to the dye-bath will set the color.

These after-mordants may change the original color while they set the dye, so run a sample test with a short length of yarn before you add the whole skein.

Vinegar

Vinegar is the work horse of natural dye procedures. It neutralizes water that is too alkaline; it acts as a solvent for certain dyes; it may help to set a color if you use it in the first rinse. Use white vinegar or acetic acid (¼ cup of vinegar equals 2 teaspoons of 99 per cent pure acetic acid). Berry dyes especially are subject to fading. Adding vinegar to increase the acidity of the dye will make the colors more permanent.

Vinegar enlarges the color range. Generally, the more vinegar, the brighter the color will be. Added to pokeberries, it reveals a beautiful red or orange-red.

Always treat the after-mordants with reserve and a discerning eye. If you use them indiscriminately, you may push a color too far and make it harsh and unattractive. Keep the process as simple as possible, letting the dye-bath do the work for you. Don't bloom the wool, then decide it is too bright and try to sadden it. If a dye does not do what you want it to do, try another dye. You can always top-dye your yarn (see page 65), or save it for another project.

Working with Handspun and Unspun Wool

There are many types of wool on the market today: 2-ply, 3-ply, 4-ply, and a variety of homespuns which range from thick to thin. All wool can be natural-dyed, and you can combine several types in weaving or needlework, and the variety of textures adds contrast and interest. Sturdy coarse wools, usually 4-ply varieties, are excellent for rugs; homespuns are good for hangings, pillows, and weaving; sweater wool works best for wearing apparel. Once you decide what you want to make, buy a style of wool that appeals to you. If the wool is very thick, mordant less than one pound at a time or increase the mordant recipe slightly. You should dye and mordant thick wool more slowly than thin wool, so that it absorbs the color evenly throughout its grist. The hotter the water, the faster the dye is absorbed into the wool, but remember that boiled wool shrinks and felts.

Most commercial wool has been washed and scoured before you buy it, and it is ready to be used for dyeing, but when you work with handspun wool or unspun fleece, you need to prepare them for the dyeing process first. Both handspun and unspun wool are highly receptive to natural dyes, and once you start using them, you will probably prefer them to any commercially prepared wool, in spite of the extra work involved. They produce deep, rich, and lovely results.

Examine the handspun wool you buy. If it feels oily when

you touch it and has an oily smell, it has only been washed and lanolin remains in it. Since lanolin is an oil and oil resists dye, you need to scour the wool before you can dye it successfully. Always skein and tie off handspun wool before you scour it.

You can purchase unspun wool in three forms: in the grease (newly shorn); washed (with some of the lanolin and impurities removed); scoured (with all impurities and oil removed).

You may dye newly shorn fleece before or after you spin it. If you decide to spin it first, wash the fleece according to the instructions below; then spin it; then scour it. The wash alone does not remove all the lanolin, but the fleece needs that lubrication in order to spin smoothly. Just don't forget to scour it before dyeing.

If you decide to dye the fleece first, you can create intriguing effects by spinning different colors together. Start by washing and then scouring the fleece. The scouring process will remove the lanolin that the wash left in, so that the wool takes the dye. Remember, though, when it comes time to spin the dyed fleece, that you need to add some lubricant, such as olive oil, to the scoured wool so that it will spin smoothly.

Regardless of which method you choose, newly shorn fleece must be washed and then scoured before dyeing. Work with a pound or less at a time; it is even better to break the pound down into smaller batches and work with them one at a time.

Washing Fleece

The highest quality wool comes from the back and shoulder areas of the sheep. Pick out the noticeably large foreign objects such as grass, twigs, or manure, if you are using britch or shank areas. While you remove them, carefully tease the wool by pulling it apart gently, a lock or so at a time, so the water will permeate each surface of the fibers.

Fill a bucket or small tub with soft, neutral water. Try for a temperature of 120-125°F. (about 49-52°C.), or as hot as you can bear to put your hand in. Immerse the fleece in water. Do not crowd the tub. It is better to wash it in small batches to avoid felting. Clean the tips of the fleece by moving your fingers towards the tips of the locks. When clean, lift the fleece from the

Illus. 47. There are many types of wool available for you to natural-dye. Remember always to dye and mordant thick wool more slowly than thin wool to ensure an even penetration (see page 49 and Illus. 40).

water and blot or roll it in a towel and squeeze to remove excess moisture. Then spread the fleece on a dry towel to air dry.

If the fleece has a high lanolin content or is very dirty, soak in a soap bath, then wash as directed above. Follow with a clear rinse. Use about one ounce of Arm and Hammer Detergent or Sal Washing Soda for two ounces of fleece. Never spray the wool or raise the bath temperature more than 10°F. (5°C.) at a time. Sudden changes in temperature will cause the wool to shrink and felt. You may add about ¼ cup vinegar to the final rinse to neutralize the wool from the alkaline residue of the soap bath.

Scouring the Wool

Method I: To one gallon of warm water, add one tablespoon of any mild soap. Wash the wool gently, being careful not to tangle it or disturb it too much. After three warm soap baths with a rinse after each bath, the wool will be scoured. Remember to add ¼ cup of vinegar to the final rinse bath.

Method II: To 4 gallons of lukewarm water, add a mild soap until the water becomes sudsy when you stir it. Immerse the wool, bring the water to a low simmer and hold it there for 15–30 minutes. Remove the wool and rinse it in water 10°F. (5°C.) cooler than the simmer bath. Rinse a second time in water 10° cooler than the first rinse, add ¼ cup of vinegar to this final rinse.

Drying Wool

To dry spun wool, simply squeeze out as much moisture as you can and hang it up to dry. To help set the spinning, tie a weight by a cord to the bottom of the skein until the wool is dry.

When you dry unspun wool, place it in any porous or mesh bag, but do not pack it so tightly as to crush the wool. Put the bag, with the wool in it, through the spin cycle of a washing machine, and then hang the bag to dry. If you don't have a washing machine available, wrap the wool in a towel to absorb the excess moisture and let it dry in a mesh bag or laid out on a towel.

Top-Dyeing

If you are dissatisfied with a color, or if you need a color you can't get from a single dye source, you may want to try top-dyeing the wool—dyeing it first in one color and then in a second. Dipping a yellow yarn, for example, into an indigo dye-bath, produces green. Black, purple and plum colors are also produced by top-dyeing. Usually you dye the wool first in the weaker color and then move to the stronger one, so that the second bath is generally very short. This process is called a "dip." When you submerge the wool in the second dye-bath, count out 20 seconds, and lift the yarn out for a color check. Dip the yarn again if you want a deeper tone.

Sectional Dyeing

After you mordant the wool, you can experiment with playful or unusual dye effects. If you knot the skein or bind it tightly in sections with cloth strips (such as cotton), you can produce a tie-dyed effect. Dye the wool in one color, untie the strips, and dye it again in a different color. The part that was

Illus. 48. Sectional dyeing will produce a tie-dyed effect.

Illus. 49. By lowering the wool into the dye in stages, you can combine several values of one color.

originally tied will absorb only the second color while the rest of the wool will exhibit the effect of the two dyes.

You can also combine several values of a single color in one skein by lowering the wool into the dye-bath in steps. The simplest way to do it is to rest a wooden dowel across the top of the dye kettle. Place the dowel through the skein; tie the wool with white cord above the dowel (as shown in Illus. 49), so that only a portion of the skein reaches into the dye-bath. After the initial section is dyed, submerge a second section in the dye-bath by simply tying the string higher, allowing more of the wool to dip into the liquid. The section you already dyed remains in the bath and will darken further while the next section is dyed. Lower the skein by moving the string as many times as you like. You might finally immerse the entire skein, or leave a section of it undyed. You can probably invent some methods of your own to make your wool unique and exciting to use.

Duplicating Color

If you need several pounds of wool all dyed the same color, gather the dyestuff all at one time if you can, and preferably from one area. Dye all the wool on the same day. As you work with a dye-bath, each successive batch of wool entered into it will come out slightly lighter. To rectify this, add some concentrate, or "ooze," to strengthen the dye after each one-pound batch, or use Glauber's salt when dyeing. For many pounds of one color, you'll probably need to do both.

Pots

If you are serious about working with natural dyes, it's a good idea to invest in several pots, one for each different mordant. If you are limited to one pot, eventually the color dulls. Of course, it is important to clean the pot thoroughly after each process, but even then a slow build-up of the mordant salts is inevitable, and the dyer always works for clear, clean colors, just as an artist does.

Enamel pots that are not chipped have little or no effect on color and are, therefore, usually used for all dye processes. The same is true of glass and stainless steel containers. As you work with natural dyes, however, you might want to experiment with some pots that do affect your final colors. Cast-iron pots, along with rusty nails and other iron articles, were used in earlier times to produce the iron mordant or to sadden a color. Before dyers had granular ferrous sulphate, the pot itself with its additives served as the mordant. Copper pots served also, because there was no sophisticated chemical called copper sulphate. Brass pots, too, were used to a purpose—generally for brighter results. You can also use this traditional procedure with the modern metal, aluminum. An aluminum pot, along with 4 teaspoons of baking soda as a mordant, yields bright results—not as bright as tin—but with this recipe you dye and mordant in a single step. As you become more experienced in working with natural dyes, you may want to experiment with pots of different metals to see what sometimes surprising and different results they produce from a single dye source.

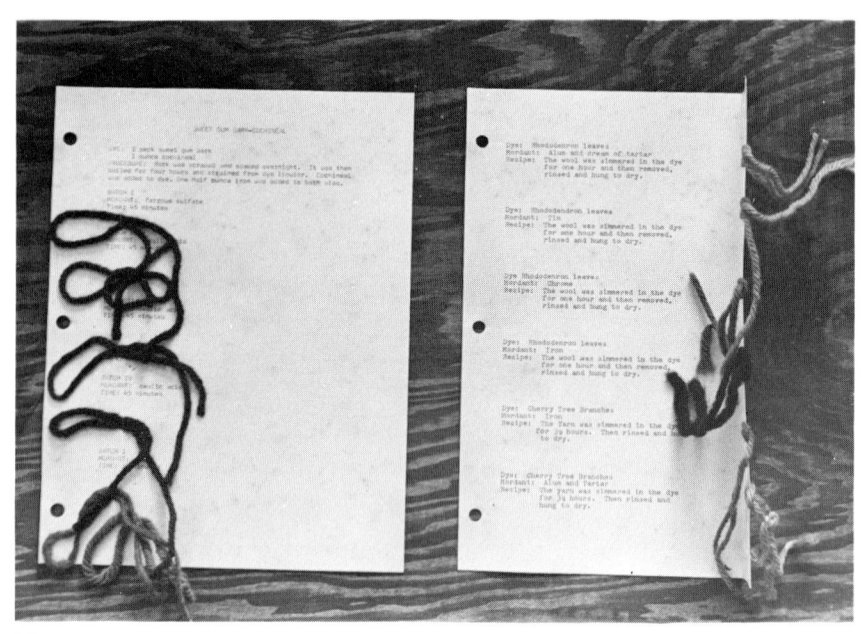

Illus. 50. Use a looseleaf notebook for your dye records so that you can add to it easily.

Notebook

You will want to snip off a strand of each batch of wool you dye to save for future reference along with a record of the recipe you used. As your samples start to accumulate, you can organize them into a diary or notebook. This private record is invaluable when you want to repeat a color or just look back to see how you created a color in one of your projects. A looseleaf notebook works well because you can add pages as you go along. Tape, staple, or tie a small wool sample to the page and, next to it, record the dyestuff, the mordant, and the recipe. If you want a more complete record, you might add the date and place where the dyestuff was collected. You may want to add a few pages for personal notes.

Group Projects with Natural Dyeing

In many ways it is easier to use natural dyes with a group of people because you can share equipment, divide the work and split costs. Mordants especially are less expensive when purchased in quantity. Old canning pots brought from attics and cellars make excellent mordant and dye kettles.

It is fun to collect dyestuff in a group, and much quicker than doing it alone. When several people pool their supply of onion peels for example, the amount multiplies much faster. You will learn to identify plants you never noticed before, and share your own knowledge of plants with others.

The set-up you need for group dyeing is much the same as when you work alone, but you'll need extra storage bins for the wool. Skeins should be tied off, tagged, labeled with the owner's name and the mordant, and then placed in bins which are labeled by mordant. A plastic dishwashing pan serves as an excellent bin; use a separate one for each mordant that you intend to use. When wool accumulates in a bin, it should be mordanted, then placed in a second bin labeled "mordanted wool" with the name of the mordant.

If more than one pound of wool is ready for a particular mordant, prepare the first pound. When it has cooled in the bath, remove it. Replenish the mordant bath by adding enough water to bring it back to its original level and half the amount that you used the first time of the mordant itself. Immerse the next pound of wool.

Since the tag on each skein records the owner's name and the mordant, it is easy to locate a skein while it is dyeing, and remove it when the color is right. At this point add the name of the dye source to the tag. With all group dyeing, it is a good idea to use the after-mordants separately, so you don't alter the condition of the dye-bath.

An outdoor clothesline is certainly the most convenient method for drying the wool, but a line in the basement works well, too. In a classroom situation, you might suspend a line across the sink area, or stretch an improvised clothesline across one section of the room with newspapers on the floor to collect the drippings. You may use drying racks, also, though they are often too small for group work.

4. Ancient Dyes— History and Recipes

Color played a dramatic rôle in early history. It warded off evil spirits, decorated bodies, and frightened enemies. In some caste systems, color indicated social position.

Since fruits, grasses, and many flowers and plants stain what they touch, it is easy to imagine how natural dyes were discovered. Simple stains were most likely rubbed directly onto people's bodies or onto crude clothing. It is not surprising to learn that natural dyes were used before 3000 B.C. Ancient Egypt, India, China, Persia, Israel, Greece, and Rome all had quite advanced dyeing methods. Traces of indigo, madder, Tyrian purple, weld, and saffron have been found in the garments of Egyptian mummies and in Greek tombs. We can even assume that dyeing was an important trade, for excavations in Pompeii exposed technically sophisticated dye shops.

Some localities became famous for their ability to produce beautiful and reliable colors. The Phoenician town of Tyre was famed for a purple dye extracted from the mucous gland of certain shellfish *(Purpura* and *Murex)*. It took 12,000 shellfish to yield one gram of the dye. Because of the elaborate extraction process, Tyrian purple represented wealth and power and became the color of kings and ecclesiastics.

Though color abounds in nature, finding ways to make it permanent has been an arduous trial and error process. Alum is one of the oldest mordants known; it was used during Egypt's Middle Kingdom in 2000 B.C. Tannin, another ancient mordant, was used both for fabrics and leather processing. A solution of sheep manure and water also served as a mordant; so did stale human urine (chamber lye); urine of the healthy male adult was preferred! Yarn was even mordanted by smoking it above the fires of certain plant and animal fibers.

By the 13th century A.D., natural dyes were used extensively throughout Europe. When European explorers discovered new lands, trade routes were set up, and dyes became a major import from Africa, Asia, China, and the West Indies. Explorers of the New World brought back with them dyes from the Incas of Peru and the Aztecs of Mexico. These civilizations provided Europe with cochineal (from insects) as well as indigo, and logwood (from plants).

In North America, the Indians, especially the Navaho and Hopi tribes, were master dyers and weavers. They knew where to gather mineral salts for mordants and produced a wide range of colors which they used on cotton for clothing, leather for footwear, and reed-like grasses for basket-making. When the Spaniards brought sheep to the New World, the Indians learned how to prepare wool and dye it.

Although the Indians adapted to the new materials and processes, American colonists clung to the dyes and methods taught them in their mother countries. They relied on imported dyes. Professional dyers, trained in Europe, were brought to America to set up dye shops. Dye imports were big business: ships from all over the world anchored in major ports with cargoes of dyes; dye peddlers travelled through rural areas; housewives, who often did their own dyeing, paid high rates for indigo and cochineal. Only the isolated householder was forced to explore the immediate surroundings for dye sources. Some early Americans tried to grow indigo, madder, weld, and woad themselves. Though the climate was suitable, their limited knowledge of growing and harvesting techniques made the products inferior to the imports.

Natural dyes were the only source of color anywhere until 1856, when an Englishman, Henry Perkins, accidentally produced mauve from coal tars, and discovered the first synthetic dye. Alizarin, a colorant for red, was developed in 1868, and soon after that, all colors were created with coal tars. These dyes took less time to use, were not affected by the seasons, and produced stable results.

Several important sources of ancient dyes are still on the market today. Some of them, not described here, such as woad (blue), weld and fustic (yellows), brazilwood, camwood, alkanet, annatto, safflower, and kermes (reds) are difficult to work with, not readily available, or tend to be fugitive in color. Others (recipes follow) are easy to find and produce beautiful results. When you purchase these dyes, be sure to store them in a dry place. Dampness weakens their potency.

Cochineal

It has always been difficult to achieve stable reds with natural dyes. When the Spaniards entered Mexico in 1518, they were amazed at the beautiful reds the Aztecs produced from what appeared to be seeds. Actually they were small insects *(Dactylopius coccus)* which fed upon certain cacti in Mexico and Guatemala. Similar in size and shape to the ladybug, these insects contain carminic acid, the principal color agent. It takes 70,000 dried insects to yield one pound of the dye, and only the mature wingless female can be used. The insects are gathered, killed in hot water and sun- or oven-dried and sometimes ground into powder. You may purchase the whole dried insect or the ground cochineal in powder form. Whether you are using the insect or the powder, the directions are the same. Cochineal was one of the principal sources of red until the end of the 19th century. You can purchase both ruby and carmine cochineal today from a natural dye supplier. They give similar results.

Cochineal is a very strong dye (wear rubber gloves when you use it); 1–1½ ounces will dye a pound of wool. Because it tends toward cool or bluish red, you need to add acid (usually vinegar or oxalic) to the dye-bath to get a brighter color. The wool will be brighter if you dye it yellow first and then top-dye in cochineal. You may also dye it first in a dye made of madder roots with an alum or tin mordant, and then top-dye it in cochineal for a bright red. For deep burgundy or plum, use an indigo dip after you dye the wool in cochineal.

In a saucepan, add 1½ ounces of whole cochineal to one cup of water; simmer until water is a deep beet color. Stir continually. This should take about 5-10 minutes. Strain the insects from the dye liquor and add this concentrate to 4 gallons of neutral water. The insects may be saved and used a second time.

If you are using the cochineal powder, simply add one ounce of powder to four gallons of neutral water. Stir.

Rose or Crimson Red

1 pound of alum-mordanted wool, wet

When the dye-bath is warm, immerse the yarn and simmer for 45 minutes or until you get the color you want. For a brighter red, add one teaspoon of table salt and 2 ounces of oxalic acid to the dye-bath, or you may add $\frac{1}{2}$ cup of vinegar to the dye.

Cardinal (Bright Red)

1 pound of tin-mordanted wool, wet

Simmer for one hour. To achieve even brighter results, add one teaspoon of table salt and $\frac{1}{2}$ ounce of oxalic acid to the dye, or you may add $\frac{1}{2}$ cup of vinegar to the dye-bath. Soap and rinse the wool after dyeing it.

Plum Red

1 pound of chrome-mordanted wool, wet

Simmer for 45 minutes. To make the color more plum-like, or increase the blue in the dye, add one tablespoon of vinegar to the dye.

Wine (Burgundy)

1 pound of iron-mordanted wool, wet

Simmer for 45 minutes.

Madder

Madder *(Rubia tinctorum)*, a plant native to Asia Minor and Europe, is one of the oldest red dyes known to man; its principal color agent is alizarin. The strongest color comes from the interior root structure of 3-year-old plants.

Madder roots produce very warm, orange-red colors. For a more primary red, use madder and then top-dye the wool with cochineal. A fast boil releases the brown color in the plant. Madder is a "substantive" dye; without a mordant, it yields a pink-tan color. It is one of the few dyes that takes well in alkaline water.

Bruise 8 ounces of madder roots with a hammer; tie them in a cheesecloth sack and soak them overnight in one quart of water. Then next morning add the cheesecloth sack and water to 4 gallons of cold water, bring it to a simmer, and hold it at that point for one hour. If you let the water boil, you will release the brown tones and the results will not be as bright. When the dye is ready, remove the cheesecloth from the bath.

RED-ORANGE

1 pound of alum-mordanted wool, wet

Immerse the wool in the warm dye-bath and simmer for one hour or until you get the color you want. You can also dye the wool by soaking it in the warm bath for several hours.

BRIGHT ORANGE

1 pound of tin-mordanted wool, wet

Simmer for one hour or until you get the orange shade you want. Give the wool a soap bath after dyeing. You can also dye the wool by soaking it for several hours in the dye-bath.

PINK-BROWN (color of faded roses)

1 pound of chrome-mordanted wool, wet

Simmer for one hour or until you get the color you want.

PURPLE-BROWN

1 pound of iron-mordanted wool, wet

Simmer for one hour, or until you get the color you want.

Logwood

Logwood dye is the heartwood of *Haematoxylon campechianum*, native to Mexico, Central America, and parts of South America. It makes beautiful offbeat blues and purples. A 12-year-old tree is ripe for the dye; the outer bark is chipped away and only the reddish heartwood selected. Logwood was used in ancient times in combination with other dyes to produce black.

Logwood extract is stronger than logwood chips; an ounce is enough to dye a pound of wool. Alkaline water (pinch of baking soda) brings out the blue quality in logwood while acid water (vinegar) turns the dye purple. As this dyebath ages it tends to give grey colors. Logwood is sensitive to light and will change in color value as it ages on the wool.

If you use the extract, simply dissolve one ounce in 4 gallons of cool water and heat. If you use the chips, tie 4 ounces in cheesecloth and let them soak overnight in one quart of water, or ripen them in the water for several days before you use them. Then add enough cold water to make 4 gallons, heat, and slowly bring to a simmer. Hold it at that point for one hour or until the dye-bath does not get any darker. If the dye does not turn a purple-blue, but remains yellow, add a pinch of baking soda to release the blue in the dye.

RED-BLUE

1 pound of alum-mordanted wool, wet

Immerse the wool in the warm dye-bath and simmer for one hour or until you get the color you want.

SILVER-BLUE/SILVER-GREY

1 pound of chrome-mordanted wool, wet

Simmer for one hour. Successive batches tend to give silver greys.

STEEL GREY-BLUE

1 pound of iron-mordanted wool

Simmer for one hour.

BRIGHT PURPLE

1 pound of tin-mordanted wool, wet

Simmer for one hour. Give the wool a soap bath after dyeing.

Indigo

Indigo *(Indigofera tinctoria)* is a shrub-like plant in the legume family and one of the most ancient sources of blue. Various species of Indigofera, native to Asia, Africa, and Central and South America, were introduced into Europe in the 16th century. One hundred pounds of leaves produces 4 ounces of indigotin, the principal color in indigo. The dye is insoluble in water and to obtain the blue color, the yarn is dipped into a special preparation or vat dye, and then left in the air to oxidize and turn blue. With a series of dips and airings you can produce the blue you want.

Indigo is one of the most exciting dyes to use and well worth making. The stock solution is the reduced indigo in concentrated form. Only a little of this solution is added to 4 gallons of water to make a dyebath or vat. As the dyebath depletes, more stock solution is added. Unused stock lasts for several days and may be used again if kept in an air-tight container.

Stock Solution

5 cups warm water (125-130°F. or 52-55°C.)
1 ounce washing soda
1 teaspoon natural indigo powder
1¼ ounce sodium dithionite (sodium hydrosulfite)

Add warm water to an enamel or glass cooking pot. Check water temperature; if it is too warm or cold the recipe won't work. Dissolve the washing soda separately in ½ cup warm water. Add to pot. The washing soda keeps the solution base so that the indigo may be reduced. Dissolve 1 teaspoon of indigo in ½ cup warm water. Gently stir into solution which should now appear blue in color. Sprinkle the sodium dithionite over the stock. Make sure you use a very dry spoon when measuring the dithionite. Read the label on the chemical carefully. Sodium dithionite loses its strength in about one year. At this point a copperlike scum should form on top of the solution. Let this sit for ½ hour. The stock should turn a yellow-green color. If it does not, sprinkle some more dithionite into the stock.

Indigo Dyebath

4 gallons warm water
1 cup stock solution
1 tablespoon sodium dithionite
drip pan, rubber gloves, wooden spoon

Sprinkle the sodium dithionite over the water and let stand for ½ hour. Slowly enter the stock solution into the water. It is imperative that the dyebath be yellow in color and the indigo stay in its reduced state. Any careless agitation will put oxygen back into the dyebath and render it useless.

Soak fibers for at least 15 minutes in warm water. When they sink, they are ready to accept the dye. Indigo works well on silk, cotton, and linen, as well as wool. Wool may first be mordanted in alum, though a mordant is not necessary when dyeing with indigo. Squeeze out excess moisture and carefully enter yarn into vat. Let sit for 3-5 minutes. Make sure the yarn is submerged in the dye at all times for even dyeing. Remove skein and hold yarn over a drip pan to air, *not* over the vat because the drips will put oxygen back into the dyebath. Turn the skein and open to expose the center so air can penetrate. Yarn will be yellow when first removed from the dye; as it oxidates the yarn will turn green and finally a light blue. Air for 5-10 minutes, or until the skein no longer darkens. Repeated dips and airings give darker shades of blue. If the vat depletes, add more stock solution. If the vat starts to turn blue, sprinkle some more sodium dithionite into the vat and wait for it to turn yellow again.

When you have a satisfactory blue, air-dry the skein. The next day rinse the yarn in a warm soap bath followed by a clear rinse. The soap will remove excess indigo from the yarn surface and avoid crocking.

Quercitron

Quercitron *(Quercus tinctoria, Quercus velutina)* is the inner bark of the black oak tree, native to North America and abundant in the Eastern United States. It is a high tannin dye that was used for yellows until the early 20th century, and it is the inner yellow cellular coat which has the strongest color. Six to 8 ounces of the wood chips will dye one pound of wool. Commercial suppliers sell a quercitron extract which is a concentrate: one ounce will dye one pound of wool. Quercitron-dyed wool, with a top-dye of indigo, produces greens.

If you are using the extract, simply dissolve one ounce in 4 gallons of water. If you are using the chips, tie them in cheesecloth and let them soak overnight in a quart of water. The next morning add the solution and cheesecloth sack to 4 gallons of cool water. Heat, bring to a simmer, and hold at that point for at least an hour or until the water does not get darker.

Yellow

1 pound of alum-mordanted wool, wet

Immerse the wool in the warm bath and simmer about 30 minutes until you get the color you want. If the color is not bright enough, bloom it, but be sure to give the wool a soap bath afterward.

Golden Yellow

1 pound of tin-mordanted wool, wet

Simmer for 30 minutes or until you get the color you want. Give the wool a soap bath after dyeing.

Mustard Yellow
1 pound of chrome-mordanted wool, wet
Simmer for 30 minutes or until you get the color you want.
Deep Mustard to Yellow-Browns
1 pound of iron-mordanted wool, wet
Simmer for 30 minutes or until you get the color you want.

Cutch or Gum Catechu

Cutch is the heartwood of *Acacia catechu* and similar species of Acacia. Native to Southeastern Asia, the Philippines and the East Indies, it was brought to Europe in the early 1800's, as an important source of brown. You need 2 ounces of catechu crystals to dye one pound of wool.

Bring to a boil in a saucepan one cup of water and 2 ounces of cutch. Stir constantly until the cutch dissolves and forms a molasses-type paste. Stir the paste into 4 gallons of hot water (be careful to use all of it) until it is fully absorbed by the water. If you add the wool before it is completely dissolved, you will get uneven results. All the mordants produce brown tones, with alum the lightest and iron the darkest.

Chocolate-Brown
4 ounces cutch
$\frac{1}{2}$ ounce copper sulphate
$\frac{1}{2}$ ounce chrome
1 pound of mordanted wool

Place dry wool in cool water and heat to a simmer. Dissolve the cutch and the copper sulphate by boiling them in a separate saucepan of water. Remove the hot yarns and add the cutch solution to the water; stir until the dye permeates the water, re-enter the yarns, remove from heat, and let the wool cool in the dye overnight. The next morning remove the yarn from the dye-bath; squeeze out excess moisture, and place it in 4 gallons of hot water mixed with the dissolved chrome. Simmer 45 minutes, rinse and dry.

Pokeweed

Pokeweed *(Phytolacca americana)* was used by North American Indians for reds and yellow-reds; home dyers in America used it as far back as the 18th century. Pokeweed is native to North

America, abundant in fields and damp woodlands in the Eastern United States. The berry cluster and stalk, which ripen in late summer and early autumn, are used for dyeing. Many dyers hesitate to use pokeberries because the dye is sensitive to light; however, it offers a wide range of colors and, in moderate light, is fairly permanent.

Crush 8 quarts of berry clusters and add them to 2 or 3 gallons of water. Keep them at a low simmer for an hour; then strain away the bulk and increase the amount of water to 4 gallons. The more vinegar you add to the dye, the redder it gets. Soak the wool in a cool bath for several hours, or keep it at a low simmer for at least a half hour. Soaking is better; when you eliminate the heat factor, you get brighter results.

PINK-YELLOW

All mordants produce degrees of this color.

Add ½ cup of vinegar to the dye-bath. Stir, immerse the wet yarn, and simmer until you get the color you want, or soak the wool in the dye for several hours.

SALMON-PINKS

All mordants produce degrees of this color.

Add one cup of vinegar to the dye-bath. Stir, enter the wet wool and simmer until you get the color you want, or soak the wool in the dye for several hours.

GARNET REDS

Alum or tin mordants give degrees of this color, but for this recipe you may eliminate the mordant completely.

Add 2 cups of vinegar to the dye-bath and simmer or soak the wool until you get the color you want. If you use unmordanted wool, simmer it in the dye for at least one hour.

Top-Dyeing to Create Black

Ancient dyers created black by combining logwood, fustic, and sumac in one bath. Black yarn for 18th century tapestries was made by first dyeing it blue, then red, and finally yellow. Using this method, you can judge the direction the color is taking and control the final results. If you want a blue-black, leave the wool in the indigo for a longer time. For red-black, leave the wool in the cochineal dye for a longer period.

It is easier to achieve black by starting with a natural wool that is not white in color.

All of the following recipes for black require an iron mordant.

BLUE-BLACK

Dye the wool first in sumac berries for deep grey; then use an indigo dip.

RED-BLACK

Dye the wool first in sumac, then use an indigo dip; finally dye the wool in cochineal. The length of time you leave the wool in the cochineal determines the warmth of the final black.

YELLOW-BLACK

Dye the wool in a strong yellow such as onion, quercitron, or fustic. Top-dye in sumac; use an indigo dip and, if necessary, return to the yellow dye.

FLAT BLACK

Dye the wool in a deep brown such as alder bark, black walnut hulls or bark, or blackberry twigs. Then use both an indigo and cochineal dip.

Top-Dyeing to Create Green

Many plants yield values of green, and you can produce green tints easily by adding some copper sulphate to yellow dye sources, but a deep green is difficult to achieve from any one source. Many dyers create their own greens by top-dyeing the wool first in a strong yellow such as apple bark, onion peels, or quercitron, and then using a blue dip, such as indigo. Use wool mordanted with alum or tin for greens.

You can create a lovely aquamarine with an alum or chrome mordant by first dyeing the wool in a light yellow source such as bamboo bark and twigs and then dipping it in cold indigo dye.

Top-Dyeing to Create Purple

Logwood with a tin mordant produces a good purple, but if you want the plum or violet range, use a chrome or iron mordant. Dye the wool first in cochineal and then top-dye it in indigo.

5. Guide to Dye Sources and Mordants

This chart provides an insight into dye sources and the colors they can produce. It is by no means complete, but merely a guide; each time you repeat a recipe or process, the colors you create will be slightly different.

Red and Purple

Dye	Botanical Name	Mordant
Alkanet (roots)	*Alkanna tinctoria*	all
Annatto (seeds)	*Bixa orellana*	all
Bloodroot (roots)	*Sanguinaria canadensis*	tin/alum
Brazilwood (bark)	*Caesalpinia echinata*	all
Camwood (bark)	*Pterocarpus sp.*	all
Cochineal (insect)	*Dactylopius coccus*	all
Lady's Bedstraw (roots)	*Galium verum*	chrome/alum/tin
Logwood (heartwood)	*Haematoxylon campechianum*	tin/alum
Lichens (all parts)	*Umbilicaria sp.*	ammonia—fermentation
Madder (root)	*Rubia tinctorum*	alum
Pokeweed (berries)	*Phytolacca americana*	alum and vinegar / tin and vinegar
Safflower (flower-heads)	*Carthamus tinctorius*	all

For purple and plum, also see sections on top-dyeing, pages 65 and 80.

Blues

Dye	Botanical Name	Mordant
Elderberries	*Sambucus nigra*	alum/chrome
Indigo (leaves)	*Indigofera tinctoria*	all
Logwood (heartwood)	*Haematoxylon campechianum*	chrome
Woad	*Isatis tinctoria*	vat dye
Spiderwort (blossoms)	*Commelinaceae sp.*	alum

Yellow

Dye	Botanical Name	Mordant
Agrimony (leaves and stalk)	*Agrimonia eupatoria*	alum
Andromeda (leaves)	*Andromeda leucothoe*	alum
Apple tree (bark)	*Pyrus (Malus) sp.*	alum

Barberry (twigs and roots)	*Berberis vulgaris*	alum
Buttercup (flower-heads)	*Ranunculus acris*	alum
Coreopsis (Calliopsis) (flower-heads)	*Coreopsis tinctoria*	alum
Dahlia (flower-heads)	*Dahlia sp.*	alum
Dandelion (flower-heads)	*Taraxacum sp.*	alum
Dock (roots and leaves)	*Rumex sp.*	alum
Dog's Mercury (entire plant except roots)	*Mercurialis perennis*	alum
Dyer's Broom (whole plant except roots)	*Genista tinctoria*	alum
Forsythia (flower-heads)	*Forsythia viridissima* or *suspensa*	alum/tin
Fustic (bark)	*Cloraphora tinctoria*	alum
Goldenrod (flowers and stalk)	*Solidago sp.*	alum
Heather (entire plant except roots)	*Calluna vulgaris*	alum
Holly (berries, bark, and leaves)	*Ilex sp.*	alum
Juniper (bark)	*Juniperus communis*	alum
Lady's Bedstraw (flowers)	*Galium verum*	alum
Marigold (flower-heads)	*Tagetes var.*	alum
Mexican Bamboo (twigs and leaves)	*Polygonum cuspidatum sp.*	alum/chrome
Mountain Laurel (leaves)	*Kalmia latifolia*	alum
Mulberry (bark)	*Morus sp.*	alum
Onion (peels)	*Allium cepa*	alum
Oaks (bark)	*Quercus sp.*	alum/tin
Osage-Orange (bark or extract)	*Maclura pomifera*	alum
Pokeweed (berries)	*Phytolacca americana*	all
Quercitron (extract)	*Quercus velutina*	alum
Rhododendron (leaves)	*Rhododendron sp.*	alum
Scotch Broom (flowers and stalk)	*Cytisus scoparius*	alum
Smartweed (entire plant except roots)	*Polygonum hydropiper*	alum
St. John's Wort (plant tops)	*Hypericum sp.*	alum
Sunflowers (flower-heads)	*Helianthus sp.*	alum
Tansy (flower-stalk)	*Tanacetum vulgare*	alum
Tomato (entire vine)	*Lycopersicon esculentum*	alum
Tulip tree (leaves)	*Liriodendron tulipifera*	alum

| Weld (leaves and seeds) | *Reseda lutea* | alum |
| Zinnia (flower-heads) | *Zinnia elegans* | alum |

Yellow-Green and Green

Dye	*Botanical Name*	*Mordant*
Birch (leaves)	*Betula sp.*	alum
Bracken (shoots)	*Pteridium aquilinum*	alum
Broom sedge (stalks and leaves)	*Andropogon virginicus*	alum
Buckthorn (berries)	*Rhamnus caroliniana*	alum
Carrot (tops)	*Daucus carota*	alum
Daffodils (flower-heads)	*Narcissus sp.*	alum
Day Lily (flower-heads)	*Hemerocallis sp.*	alum
Lily of the Valley (leaves)	*Convallaria majalis*	alum
Nettle (entire plant except roots)	*Urtica dioica*	alum
Onion grass—wild (tops)	*Allium cepa sp.*	alum/tin/chrome
Poplar (leaves)	*Populus sp.*	alum
Queen Anne's Lace (Wild Carrot) (flower-stalk)	*Daucus carota*	alum
Queen of the Meadow (plant top)	*Filipendula ulmaria*	alum
Rhododendron (leaves)	*Rhododendron sp.*	alum bloomed tin chrome bloomed
Ragweed (entire plant except roots)	*Ambrosia sp.*	alum
Sedge (stalk)	*Cyperaceae sp.*	alum
Smartweed (entire plant except roots)	*Polygonum hydropiper*	alum
Solomon's Seal (leaves)	*Polygonatum sp.*	alum
Spinach (leaves)	*Spinacia oleracea*	alum
Tansy (flower-heads)	*Tanacetum vulgare*	alum
Yarrow (entire plant except roots)	*Achillea millefolium*	iron

Top-dyeing from yellow to blue, or greening any yellow dye with copper sulphate, will also produce green.

Orange and Gold

Dye	*Botanical Name*	*Mordant*
Agrimony (leaves and stalk)	*Agrimonia eupatoria*	chrome
Apple tree (bark)	*Pyrus (Malus) sp.*	tin/chrome

Dye	Botanical Name	Mordant
Coreopsis (Calliopsis) (flower-heads)	*Coreopsis tinctoria*	tin/chrome
Dahlia (flower-heads)	*Dahlia sp.*	chrome
Dandelion (flower-heads)	*Taraxacum sp.*	tin
Dock (roots)	*Rumex obtusifolius*	tin
Goldenrod (flower-stalk)	*Solidago sp.*	tin
Lady's Bedstraw (roots)	*Galium verum*	tin
Madder (roots)	*Rubia tinctorum*	tin
Marigold (flower-heads)	*Tagetes var.*	tin/chrome
Mulberry (bark)	*Morus sp.*	tin
Oaks (bark)	*Quercus sp.*	tin/chrome
Onion (peels)	*Allium cepa*	tin
Quercitron (extract)	*Quercus velutina*	tin
Sunflowers (flower-heads)	*Helianthus sp.*	tin
Tulip tree (leaves)	*Liriodendron tulipifera*	tin
Willow (bark and twigs)	*Salix sp.*	tin
Zinnia (flower-heads)	*Zinnia elegans*	tin

Ochre
Dye	Botanical Name	Mordant
Apple tree (bark)	*Pyrus (Malus) sp.*	chrome
Broom sedge (stalk and leaves)	*Andropogon virginicus*	chrome
Day Lily (flower-heads)	*Hemerocallis sp.*	chrome
Goldenrod (flower-heads)	*Solidago sp.*	chrome
Marigold (flower-heads)	*Tagetes var.*	chrome
Mountain Laurel (leaves)	*Kalmia latifolia*	chrome
Mulberry (bark)	*Morus sp.*	chrome
Onion (peels)	*Allium cepa*	chrome
Osage Orange (bark)	*Maclura pomifera*	chrome
Poplar (leaves)	*Populus sp.*	chrome
Privet (leaves)	*Ligustrum vulgare*	chrome
Quercitron (extract)	*Quercus velutina*	chrome
Smartweed (entire plant except roots)	*Polygonum hydropiper*	chrome

Brown and Tan
Dye	Botanical Name	Mordant
Acorns	All *Quercus sp.*	all
Alders (bark)	*Alnus sp.*	all
Apple tree (bark)	*Pyrus (Malus) sp.*	iron
Ash (bark)	*Fraxinus sp.*	all
Beech (bark)	*Fagus sp.*	all

Dye	Botanical Name	Mordant
Birch (bark)	Betula sp.	all
Blackberry (twigs)	Rubus sp.	iron
Black Walnut (hulls and bark)	Juglans nigra	all
Buckthorn (berries)	Rhamnus caroliniana	iron
Butternut (hulls)	Juglans cinerea	all
Cherry tree (bark)	Prunus sp.	all
Coffee (beans or ground)	Coffea arabica	all
Cutch (heartwood)	Acacia catechu	all
Dandelion (roots)	Taraxacum sp.	all
Dock (roots)	Rumex obtusifolius	chrome/iron
English Walnut (hulls)	Juglans regia	all
Grape (roots)	Vitis rotundifolia	all
Hemlock (bark)	Tsuga canadensis	alum/chrome/iron
Hickory nut (hulls)	Carya sp.	all
Horse Chestnut (hulls)	Aesculus hippocastanum	all
Lombardy Poplar (leaves)	Populus nigra	chrome/iron
Maples (bark)	Acer sp.	all
Oaks (bark)	Quercus sp.	iron
Pecan (hulls)	Carya sp.	all
Pine cones (all species)	Pinus sp.	all
Privet (clippings)	Ligustrum vulgare	iron
Sassafras (bark)	Sassafras albidum	chrome/iron
Sumac (berries and twigs)	Rhus sp.	all
Tea (leaves)	Thea sinensis	all
Willow (bark)	Salix sp.	all

Grey

Dye	Botanical Name	Mordant
Bayberry (leaves)	Myrica pennsylvanica	alum saddened
Blackberry (shoots)	Rubus sp.	alum saddened
Buckthorn (berries)	Rhamnus caroliniana	alum
Horse Chestnut (bark)	Aesculus hippocastanum	alum saddened
Ivy (berries)	Hedera sp.	alum saddened
Logwood (heartwood)	Haematoxylon campechianum	iron/chrome
Mountain Laurel (leaves)	Kalmia latifolia	iron
Rhododendron (leaves)	Rhododendron sp.	iron
Sumac (berries)	Rhus sp.	iron/alum saddened
Sweet Gum (balls)	Liquidambar styraciflua	iron/alum saddened
Tea (leaves)	Thea sinensis	chrome/iron

Glossary

acetic acid—weak acid found in vinegar. Use it to neutralize alkaline water, develop color potential of berry dyes, and help set colors after dyeing. One-fourth cup white vinegar equals two teaspoons 99% pure acetic acid.

adjective—natural dyes that need a mordant to fix the dye permanently to the fiber.

alum—aluminum potassium sulphate, aluminum ammonium sulphate.

blooming—a process which brightens colors by the use of stannous chloride. It is usually done at the midpoint of dyeing and is followed by a soap bath.

chrome—bichromate of potash, potassium dichromate, potassium bichromate.

copper sulphate—bluestone, blue vitriol.

cream of tartar—agrol, tartaric acid.

crock—the rubbing-off of a dye from the wool, caused by improper rinse or mordanting.

cutch—important source of brown dye from the heartwood of the *Acacia catechu* and similar species of *Acacia*.

dye-bath—the dye liquor diluted with water to equal 4 gallons of liquid.

dye liquor—the concentrated natural dye; the "ooze."

dye source—plant or animal source capable of producing a natural dye.

dyestuff—the gathered material to be used in making a natural dye.

enter—to immerse the yarn in the dye or mordant bath.

felt—matting of the wool, caused by sudden temperature change, fast boiling, or over-agitation during one of the processes.

fugitive—dyes that fade quickly and cannot be fixed permanently on the wool, even with the use of mordants.

Glauber's salt—hydrated sodium sulphate.

greening—a process which brings out the green tones of a dye, by adding copper sulphate to the dye-bath, usually at the midpoint of dyeing; commonly used with yellow dyes.

grist—the thickness of a strand of wool.

hydrochloric acid—muriatic acid, spirit of salt.

in the grease—a fresh fleece; wool that has the lanolin of the sheep still in it.

iron—copperas, green vitriol, ferrous sulphate.

mordant—mineral salt which fixes the dye on the wool and makes the color permanent.

natural dye—a dye obtained from a plant or an animal source.

ooze—a concentrated natural dye; the dye liquor.

saddening—a process which darkens colors by the use of ferrous sulphate, usually applied at the midpoint of dyeing; also called stuffing.

scour—remove all impurities from the wool.

sectional dyeing—dyeing only a section of the skein at a time in order to produce unusual effects.

simmer—a pre-boil state ranging from 170° to 190° F. (77° to 88° C.).

skein—a hank of yarn; yarn arranged in an oval so that it may be mordanted and dyed.

sodium benzoate—a white, odorless granule or powder, used as a preservative and especially effective with slightly acid dyes. When you add one teaspoon of it to a gallon of dye, the dye will last for several months in an air-tight container.

spent—dye-bath exhausted of its color.

substantive—natural dyes which color yarns permanently without need of mordants.

sulphuric acid—oil of vitriol.

tie-dye—tightly binding sections of a skein of yarn so they cannot absorb the dye; produces a variegated effect.

tie-off—the securing of the skein of yarn with some non-shrinking white cord; usually, the wool is tied off in four places; the tie-off should be tight enough to prevent the wool from tangling, but free enough to let the mordant and dye penetrate.

tin—stannous chloride.

top-dyeing—dyeing one color over another.

vinegar—diluted acetic acid.

washed wool—wool from which most impurities have been removed, but which has some remaining lanolin.

working the wool—turning, exposing, or moving the wool in a back-and-forth motion while it is in the mordant or dye-bath, to ensure even penetration.

Suppliers

All suppliers listed are willing to fill small orders from individuals. When you request free catalogues, please enclose stamped self-addressed envelope.

In the United States:

*Owl & Olive Weavers
704 29th St. South
Birmingham, Al. 35233

*Hidden Village
215 Yale Ave.
Claremont, Ca. 91711

The Camel
935 G St.
Arcata, Ca. 95521
   yarn, fleece, weaving
   and spinning supplies

*Custom Handweavers
Allied Arts Guild
Arbor Rd. & Creek Dr.
Menlo Park, Ca. 94025
   free catalogue

The Mercantile
P.O. Box 343
Berkeley, Ca. 94701
   natural dyes, mordants,
   weaving and spinning
   supplies, free catalogue

*Straw Into Gold
P.O. Box 2904
5509 College Ave.
Oakland, Ca. 94618

*All supplies: natural dyes, mordants, yarn, fleece, weaving and spinning supplies

Nature's Herb Company
281 Ellis St.
San Francisco, Ca. 94102
   natural dyes

*Sheep Village
2005 Bridgeway
Sausalito, Ca. 94965

*The Handweaver
460 First St. East
Sonoma, Ca. 95476
   free catalogue

Colonial Textiles
82 Plants Dam Road
East Lyme, Ct. 06333
   natural dyes, mordants,
   fleece, spinning supplies,
   free catalogue

*Serendipity Shop
1547 Ellinwood
Des Plaines, Il. 60016
   free catalogue

*The Yarn Barn
Box 334
730 Massachusetts
Lawrence, Ka. 66044

*Earth Guild/Grateful Union
15 Tudor Street
Cambridge, Ma. 02139

*Traditional Handicrafts
571 Randolph St.
Northville, Mi. 48167
   free catalogue

*The Yarnery,
1648 Grand Ave.
St. Paul, Mn. 55105

Depth of Field Inc.
405 Cedar Ave.
Minneapolis, Mn. 55404
   natural dyes, mordants,
   yarn, weaving and
   spinning supplies,
   free catalogue

*Village Wools
   Fibrecraft Materials and
   Supplies
308 San Felipe, N.W.
Albuquerque, N.M. 87104

Kem Chemical Co.
545 S. Fulton St.
Mount Vernon, N.Y. 10550
   mordants, free price list

Coulter Studios
118 E. 59th St.
New York, N.Y. 10022
   yarn, fleece, weaving and
   spinning supplies

The Spinster
34 Hamilton Ave.
Sloatsburg, N.Y. 10974
   natural dyes, mordants,
   yarn, fleece, spinning
   supplies, free catalogue

*Blacksheep Weaving and
Craft Supply
315 S.W. 3rd St.
Corvallis, Or. 97330
   free catalogue

*Wildflower Fibers
211 N.W. Davis St.
Portland, Or. 97209
   free price list

*Gordon's Naturals
P.O. Box 506
Roseburg, Or. 97470

*Lenos Handcrafts
2037 Walnut St.
Philadelphia, Pa. 19103

*Craft Industries
1513 and 1516 W. Alabama
Houston, Tx. 77006

*Intertwine
217 Trolley Square
Salt Lake City, Ut. 84102
   free catalogue

*Tapestry
4176 Meridian Rd.
Bellingham, Wa. 98225
   free catalogue

Weaving Works
5049 Brooklyn Ave.
Seattle, Wa. 98105
   yarn, fleece, weaving
   and spinning supplies,
   free catalogue

Handweavers Guild of America, Inc.
998 Farmington Ave.
West Hartford, Conn. 06107
   a non-profit organization, prepares
   the magazine
   Shuttle, Spindle & Dyepot
   and other publications,
   including a suppliers directory of
   materials and equipment for dyers,
   spinners, and weavers ($2.00 U.S.).

In Canada:

*Gina Brown Needlecraft
 Studio
 1230 17th Ave., Calgary S.W.
 Alberta T2T OB, Canada

*Coquitlam Crafts
 946B Brunette Ave.
 Maillardville V3K 1C9,
 Coquitlam, B.C. Canada
   free catalogue

*Northwest Handcraft House
 110 West Esplanade
 Vancouver, B.C. V7M/1A2
 Canada

*Nostalgia Craft Supplies
 5739 Granville St.
 Vancouver, B.C. Canada

Wide World of Herbs, Ltd.
11 St. Catherine St. East
Montreal, Que.
   natural dyes, mordants

In England:

Comak Chemicals Ltd.
Swinton Works
Moon St.
London N.1, England

In Australia:

C. D. FitzHardinge-Bailey
St. Aubyn
15 Dutton St.
Bankstown, N.S.W. 2200
Australia

Spinners and Weavers' Supplies
P.O. Box 56 Woollahra
N.S.W. 2025
Sydney, Australia

In Greece:

Stavros Kouyoumoutzakis
Workshop Spun Wools
166 Kalokerinou Ave.
Iraklion, Crete, Greece

In New Zealand:

Local pharmacists sell mordants.

93

Metric Conversions

U.S. Measure   *Metric (approx.)*

1 ounce (fluid) . . . . .   30 milliliters

1 ounce (weight) . . . .   28 grams

1 pound or 16 ounces . . .   454 grams or .454 kilogram

1 quart . . . .   0.95 liter

5 U.S. gallons. . . . . .   4 Imperial gallons (12 liters)

4 U.S. gallons. . . . . .   15.2 liters

1 U.S. gallon . . . . . .   3.8 liters

1 cup . . . .   240 milliliters

1 peck . . . .   8.75 liters

1 inch . . . .   25 mm. or 2.5 cm.

INDEX

acetic acid, 60, 86
adjective dyes, 48, 86
after-mordants, 56, 57, 60, 69
alder bark, 29, 80
alizarin, 71, 73
alkanet, 71
alum, 9, 17, 32, 34, 60, 70, 72, 73, 74, 75, 76, 77, 78, 79, 80-85
aluminum, 67
ancient dyes, history of, 70-80
annatto, 71
anthrocyanins, 11
apple peels, 49
apple tree bark, 29, 46, 80
backings, 43
backstitch sewing, 23
baking soda, 31, 67, 75
barks, 24, 25, 26, 27, 29, 30, 74
batches, 40, 41
beet roots, 49
blackberry twigs, 79
black walnut hulls, 29, 48, 80
blooming, 56, 57, 61, 77, 86
blueberries, 49
borax, 31
brazilwood, 71
britch area, 62
bruising, 16, 30, 73
bulk material, 10, 13
camwood, 71
carminic acid, 72
cheesecloth, 9, 13, 14, 73, 74
chrome (potassium dichromate), 32, 34, 60, 85
chrome mordant, 33, 34, 73, 74, 75, 78, 80
cochineal, 71, 72, 79, 80
coffee, 10, 13, 14
colander, 9
collecting cones and hulls, 27-29
collecting roots, 27, 28
cones, 27, 29, 30
copper sulphate, 57, 60, 67, 78, 79, 86
cream of tartar, 9, 17, 32, 34, 35, 57, 86
crock, 22, 33, 86
cutch catechu, 78, 87
dandelion flower-heads, 10, 15-16, 56
dandelion roots, 27, 29
dipping, 65
drying, 64, 69
dye-bath, 10, 20, 21, 25, 32
dye extraction time, 11, 12, 14-15
dye imports, 71
dyeing the wool, 21
dyeing time, 40
dye liquor, 10, 14, 17, 20, 21, 40, 87
dyematter, 10, 26
dye recipes, 14, 29, 40, 72-80

dye sources, 10-11, 25, 29, 40, 69, 71-72, 81-85, 87
  blues, 81
  brown and tan, 84
  grey, 84-85
  ochre, 83
  orange and gold, 83
  red and purple, 81
  yellow, 81-83
  yellow-green and green, 83
dyestuff, 9, 13, 14, 25, 27, 30, 39, 87
  collecting, 69
  freezing, 55-56
  storing and selecting, 53-56
enamel kettle, 9, 31, 67
entering, 87
equipment, 7, 9
fade test, 52
felting (matting), 20, 87
frame loom, 23
fugitive sources, 49, 52, 72, 74, 87
fustic, 71, 79, 80
Glauber's salt, 57-60, 67, 87
glossary, 86-89
goldenrod, storing of, 56
grease wool, 62, 88
greening, 57, 87
grist, 87
group projects, 68-69
gum catechu, see cutch catechu
handspun wool, 61, 64
hanks, 19, 33
heat sources, 9
hickory nut hulls, 29
homespun wool, 61
hooked rug, 41-47
hulls, 28, 29
hydrochloric acid, 60, 88
indicator package, 31
indicator paper, 9, 31
indigo, 65, 70, 71, 75-77, 79, 80
indigotin, 75
iron (ferrous sulphate), 32, 35, 57, 60, 67, 88
iron mordant, 35, 67, 73, 74, 75, 78, 80
kermes, 72
knot system, 36
labels, 36, 69
lanolin, 62, 64
leather, 70, 71
lichens, 48
litmus paper, 31
logwood, 71, 74-75
macrame, 23
madder, 70, 71, 73-74
manure, 62, 70
marigold flower-heads, 10, 15-16
mauve, 71

95

measuring cup, 9
mordant bath, 34, 35, 36
mordanting, 32, 34–35, 61, 69
mordant procedure, 36
mordant recipes, 17, 25, 33, 34–35
mordants, 17, 21, 25, 32, 33, 34–35, 36, 41, 70, 81–85, 88
mordant salts, 67
Murex, 70
muslin sack, 13, 14
natural dye, 88
natural fibers, 19
notebook, 68
olive oil, 62
onion dye, 14, 33, 80
onion grass, 10, 14–15
onion peels, 10, 11, 48, 57, 80
"ooze," 40, 67, 88
oxalic acid, 35, 72, 73
oxidation, 33, 76
Perkins, Henry, 71
pH factor, 32
pine cones, 7, 29
pokeberries, 61
pokeweed, 78–79
pots, 67
preparing dyes, 13, 14, 15, 29–30
preparing the dyestuff and dye liquor, 11–13
preparing the dye-bath, 20
preserving dyes, 56
pruning, 26
Purpura, 70
quercitron, 77–78, 80
red onions, 14
rhododendron leaves, 10, 14–15, 48, 49
Rhus glabra, 16
Rhus typhina, 16
Rhus vernix, 16
rinse bucket, 9
rinsing, 21–22
roots, 25, 27, 28, 30
rose petals, 49
rubber gloves, 9, 72, 76
rug hookers, 42, 44
saddening, 57, 61, 67, 88
safflower, 72
saffron, 70
scale, 9
scoured wool, 62
scouring, 61, 62, 64, 88

sectional dyeing, 65, 88, 89
setting, 60
shank area, 62
simmer, 88
skeins, 19, 33, 88
smoking yarns, 71
soaking, 14, 15, 20, 21, 30, 41, 74, 75, 79
sodium benzoate, 56, 88
soumak weave, 23
spent, 89
spinach leaves, 10, 14–15
spinning, 62, 64
strainer, 9, 14
substantive dyes, 48, 73, 89
sulphuric acid, 89
sumac, 10, 13, 16, 79, 80
supplies, 90–93
sweet gum balls, 29, 30
synthetic dyes, 71–72
synthetic fibers, 19
tabby weave, 23
tag system, 36–40, 52, 69
tannin, 14, 16, 25, 60, 70, 77
tea, 10, 13, 14
terminology, 10
thermometer, 9, 21
tie-dyeing (sectional dyeing), 65, 88, 89
tie-off, 89
tin (stannous chloride) 32, 35, 56, 60, 67, 89
tin mordant, 33, 35, 73, 74, 75, 77, 80
tints, 41
top-dyeing, 61, 65, 72, 77, 79–80, 89
"tree wound paint," 26
tumeric, 49
Tyrian purple, 70
unspun wool, 61
urine, 70–71
vat dye, 75
vinegar, 31, 60–61, 64, 72, 73, 79, 89
warp, 23
washing fleece, 62, 89
wash test, 53
water, 10, 30–32
water, mineral content of, 10, 32
water, neutralizing, 10, 31, 60
weft, 23
weld, 70, 71, 72
willow bark, 29
woad, 71, 72
working the wool, 89